César Chávez

A Voice for Farmworkers

BÁRBARA C. CRUZ

Enslow Publishers, Inc.

40 Industrial Road   PO Box 38
Box 398   Aldershot
Berkeley Heights, NJ 07922   Hants GU12 6BP
USA   UK

http://www.enslow.com

Para mis padres, Ignacio y Elsa Acosta,
gran trabajadores y seres humanos.

Library of Congress Cataloging-in-Publication Data

Cruz, Bárbara.
    César Chávez : a voice for farmworkers / Bárbara C. Cruz.
      p. cm. — (Latino biography library)
    Includes bibliographical references and index.
    ISBN 0-7660-2489-X (hardcover)
    1. Chavez, Cesar, 1927— -Juvenile literature. 2. Labor leaders—United States—Biography—Juvenile literature. 3. Migrant agricultural laborers—United States—Biography—Juvenile literature. 4. Mexican Americans—Biography—Juvenile literature. 5. United Farmworkers—History—Juvenile literature. I. Title. II. Series.
    HD6509.C48C78 2005
    331.88'13'092—dc22

                                2004027538

Printed in the United States of America

10 9 8 7 6 5 4 3 2 1

To Our Readers: We have done our best to make sure all Internet Addresses in this book were active and appropriate when we went to press. However, the author and the publisher have no control over and assume no liability for the material available on those Internet sites or on other Web sites they may link to. Any comments or suggestions can be sent by e-mail to comments@enslow.com or to the address on the back cover.

Every effort has been made to locate all copyright holders of material used in this book. If any errors or omissions have occurred, corrections will be made in future editions of this book.

Illustration Credits: AP/Wide World, pp. 1, 3, 4, 7, 21, 23, 24, 25, 59, 62, 63, 71, 76–77, 78, 82, 85, 88, 91, 93, 95, 98, 102–103, 105, 109, 110; Cesar E. Chavez Foundation, pp. 10, 13, 15, 28, 30, 32, 34, 35, 39; Enslow Publishers, Inc., pp. 20, 27; Library of Congress, p. 19; Walter P. Reuther Library, Wayne State University, pp. 9, 16, 40, 43, 46, 48, 53, 64, 67, 69, 75, 87.

Cover Illustration: AP/Wide World.

Contents

César Chávez

1

"A Living Saint"

César Chávez knew that something dramatic needed to be done to call attention to the plight of migrant farmworkers. Their pay was meager. Many lived in labor camps in cramped quarters, perhaps ten or more people in a trailer home. Often their housing had no bathrooms, no electricity, and no running water. Chávez had been a migrant farm laborer at one time, and he knew firsthand how hard the workers' lives could be.

Chávez was the leader of the United Farmworkers of America (UFW), a union he had created to help improve conditions for the migrants. Like other labor unions, the UFW was an association that represented the rights of workers. At this time, the union was involved in an effort to help the people who picked grapes. Despite a number of peaceful protests led by the UFW over the past three years, the growers who hired the pickers remained unwilling to negotiate for better conditions. The growers increasingly met the workers' demands with violence, and Chávez worried that the workers would end up retaliating with violence. He did not want that to happen.

On February 14, 1968, the UFW called for a meeting. Chávez announced that he had begun a fast. Migrant farmworkers and their families were suffering. He was fasting to call attention to the desperate conditions of their lives.[1] He had stopped eating as a pledge of his commitment to nonviolent protest.

As soon as he made the announcement, Chávez left the meeting hall and walked to the union's headquarters, called Forty Acres. The complex included union

Fasting

Fasting means going without food for a stretch of time. The morning meal of breakfast, for example, refers to breaking one's overnight fast. People fast for a variety of reasons. Some are seeking health, spiritual, or political goals. Many religions call for a time of fasting to mark atonement, renewal, sorrow, or spiritual uplift. Political protesters have fasted to show commitment to their cause and dedication to nonviolence.

César Chávez fasted both for spiritual reasons and to call attention to the plight of the farmworkers. His refusal to eat was an effective political strategy. Many people were impressed by the strength of his beliefs—that he would sacrifice his own health for the welfare of the migrant workers. This fast was the first of several that Chávez would carry out over the next twenty-five years.

offices, a medical clinic, and a gas station. It was at the gas station that his drama would unfold.

Chávez set up an area for himself in the storage room of the gas station. There he placed a simple cot and a few religious items. Chávez continued to conduct the business of the union, but he spent most of his time in bed to save energy. A daily mass was held each evening. Hundreds of farmworkers and their families showed up every day to attend mass, to meet Chávez, and to express their support

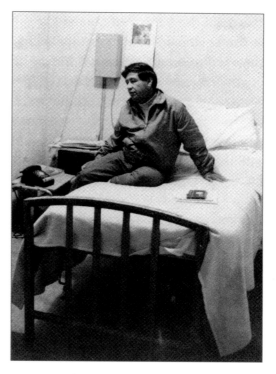

For Chávez, fasting did not put a halt to union business—he worked from his bed.

and admiration. They pitched tents and waited in line for a chance to speak with Chávez. Although Chávez refused to talk to reporters, he welcomed the visiting *campesinos* (farmworkers) into the cramped room.

Thousands of people traveled to Forty Acres during Chávez's fast. Government officials, religious leaders, and civilians from all walks of life learned of his fast and showed their support. When Dr. Martin Luther King, Jr., the prominent civil rights leader, heard about

Chávez's fast, he sent a telegram wishing Chávez success in his fight for justice. Dr. King, too, was a staunch believer in nonviolence.

The fast was not easy for Chávez. He suffered from intense hunger pains, headaches, pain in his joints, and nightmares about food. Finally, after a couple of weeks, the nightmares and cravings went away and Chávez learned to cope with the physical hardships. People reported that when Chávez fasted, "he thought and spoke with great clarity."[2]

As the days wore on, Chávez was pressured by many of his supporters to call an end to the fast. "What will happen to the cause," they asked, "if you die?" Senator Robert Kennedy of New York, who had praised Chávez's commitment, now sent a telegram asking him to reconsider.

Twenty-five days later, Chávez finally ended his fast at the insistence of his doctors. He had lost thirty-five pounds. Chávez asked to break his fast with a mass at a local park and invited Senator Kennedy, a fellow Catholic, to attend the service. More than four thousand farmworkers came to the mass. They watched as Chávez broke his fast by eating a piece of bread. Awed by Chávez's steadfast determination, Senator Kennedy called him "a living saint."[3]

Although Chávez was too weak to stand or speak, a statement he had written was read in both Spanish and English. Reporters and television cameras recorded the moving message:

Senator Robert Kennedy and Helen Chávez sat with César as he broke his fast with a small piece of bread.

> Our struggle is not easy. Those who oppose our cause are rich and powerful, and they have many allies in high places. We are poor. Our allies are few. But we have something the rich do not own. We have our own bodies and spirits and the justice of our cause as our weapons.[4]

Chávez's fast was very effective in calling national attention to the plight of the farmworkers. The public responded by not buying table grapes. By 1969, almost three-quarters of the California grape growers were out of business. By the spring of 1970, the remaining growers and the UFW finally signed an agreement.

César looks like a happy little baby at his baptism.

Growing Up

César Chávez was named after his grandfather Cesario, who was known as Papa Chayo in the family. Papa Chayo had escaped from one of the biggest *haciendas* (ranches) in Mexico in the 1880s. At that time, the conditions for workers on these large plantations resembled slavery. Babies' expenses for food, clothing, and shelter were carefully noted by the ranch owner from the time they were born. These costs were recorded in a book. By the time the babies grew into children old enough to work, they were already in debt. They would have to spend the rest of their lives paying back the hacienda owners. Every year, some of their debt was worked off— but more was logged in for that year's expenses. It was impossible to get free of the system. Papa Chayo did not want to spend his life as a worker on the hacienda where he had been born.

As a young man, Papa Chayo ran away from the

hacienda and crossed the border into the United States. He settled in the Gila Valley of Arizona, where he met and married Dorotea. Orphaned as a child, Dorotea had been raised in a convent. The nuns there taught her how to read and write in Spanish and in Latin. She would later share these lessons with her children and then her grandchildren, who called her Mama Tella. She was devoutly Catholic and impressed the importance of that religion on her family.

Papa Chayo and Mama Tella eventually had fifteen children. One by one, the children grew up and left home. Only their son Librado stayed to work on the family farm. In 1924, Librado married Juana Estrada, and over time the couple bought a garage, a pool hall, and a grocery store. It was there that César Estrada Chávez was born on March 31, 1927. He was the second of their six children.

Juana Chávez taught her life values to César and her other children. She repeated the *dichos* (sayings or proverbs) that she had learned herself as a child. Many of them had to do with the importance of resolving problems peacefully, without fighting. César later recalled her saying, "It takes two to fight; one can't do it alone." Or she would declare, "It's better to say that he ran from here than to say he died here."[1] She also stressed the importance of sharing and the value of self-sacrifice. Because there was no church nearby, César's mother and grandmother taught the children their prayers and how to practice their religion.

Later, the Chávez children would recall their childhood years fondly. Although everyone helped in the family business, the children attended school and had plenty of time to play. César and his younger brother Richard loved playing billiard games in the family's pool hall.

Many friends and relatives bought their groceries and other provisions at the Chávez store. Often, Librado gave his customers the items they needed on credit, trusting that they would pay him later. For a few years, this arrangement worked. The Chávezes were able to make a good living. Then, in 1929, the Great Depression changed the family's modest but comfortable lifestyle forever.

The Great Depression lasted from 1929 to about 1940. As people used up their savings, charities strained to provide life's basic necessities for the thousands of suddenly impoverished families.

The Great Depression greatly affected César's family. César later said it was his father's generosity that eventually became his undoing. Customers who had been able to honor their debts found

César and his older sister, Rita.

themselves destitute and unable to pay Librado for their groceries. César recalled, "There were too many relatives, too many mouths to feed. . . . It wasn't long before he had given all his store out in credit."[2]

In 1932, Librado was forced to sell his business. The family moved in with Librado's parents. Space was very limited in the adobe house shared by the Chávez clan, but the family was luckier than many others, which had been even harder hit by the depression. Unlike those who lived in cities, the Chávez family had access to fresh

The Great Depression

After the difficult years of World War I, many citizens in the United States enjoyed newfound prosperity. But the booming economy of the seemingly carefree 1920s was dealt a hard blow on October 29, 1929, when the stock market crashed. As investors lost millions of dollars, the effects were immediately felt throughout the country and, eventually, the world. Businesses and banks closed. Thousands of people lost their jobs and their homes. With so much poverty, public assistance programs tried to help. Soup kitchens, providing meager but nutritious meals to the needy, cropped up in many towns.

At the same time, the American Midwest began to suffer from one of the worst droughts in history. The plains region became known as the Dust Bowl when destructive dust storms wrecked crops, injured people and livestock, and ruined property. Many families packed up their few belongings and headed to California in search of a better life.

César and Rita dressed up in their very best clothes for their First Communion.

César's grandfather built his adobe house in the Gila Valley in Arizona. Years later, only some of these clay bricks remained.

eggs, milk, and vegetables they grew themselves. They even had enough food to share with the migrant workers who passed through the area.

For the next five years, everyone in the Chávez family worked on the farm, raising crops and livestock. But farming in hot, dry Arizona was a challenge, made almost impossible when the drought of 1933 dried up even the Colorado River.

When César was ten, at the height of the Great Depression, his family lost the farm. The back taxes on the land had been steadily increasing over the years until the bill reached several thousand dollars. César's parents had no way to pay the bill when it came due in 1937. Sadly, Mama Tella died that year as well. The family packed their car with as many of their belongings as it would hold, but much of it did not fit. "We left everything behind," said César later. "Left chickens and cows and horses and all the implements. Things belonging to my father's family and my mother's as well. Everything."[3]

At the time, there were not many jobs, especially for ethnic minorities such as African Americans and Mexican Americans. Librado heard that there were farm jobs to be had in California picking crops. So, like thousands of others, the family left their home and moved to California in search of employment. César's family became migrant farmworkers. It would prove to be a very different lifestyle from what the family had been accustomed to.

Migrant Life

Adjusting to their new lives as migrant workers was difficult for the Chávez clan. Migrant workers travel from place to place in search of employment. The children, who had been used to running freely around their sprawling farm, resented the fences, the noise, and the crowding in California. On the farm in Arizona, César said, "we had a special place we would play, by this tree that was our own. And when we built things—playhouses, bridges, barns—we could come back the next day and they would be there."[1] Everything was different in California, where a ball left outside could disappear in an instant.

This was also a time when ethnic groups were often treated as second-class citizens. Movie theaters, schools, neighborhoods, and the military were segregated. Throughout the Southwest, businesses prominently displayed signs that said NO DOGS OR MEXICANS ALLOWED or

During the Great Depression, many people had to load up their possessions and leave their homes in search of work.

White Trade Only, meaning that only white customers were welcomed. In some communities, the public skating rinks, pools, and parks allowed Mexican Americans to use the facilities on only one day a week. In California one morning, César accompanied his father into a run-down diner to buy some coffee. They were ordered to leave because the restaurant served only white customers. Years later, César could still recall the deeply pained expression on his father's face.[2]

Eventually, the Chávez family traveled from Sacramento in northern California to the Imperial

Valley in the south. César's parents followed the harvest of different fruits and vegetables, settling for a short time wherever a crop was ripe and ready for picking. Chávez attended more than thirty-five different elementary schools as they moved from place to place. In some communities, Mexican children were not allowed to attend schools with white children. The Chávez children actually preferred the segregated schools because they

Racism and Segregation

Racism is the belief that people of different races or ethnic backgrounds have distinct differences, and that some races are better than others. Racists consider their own race to be superior—smarter, stronger, more virtuous—and they use this belief to justify keeping racial or ethnic groups apart. Separation of the races, called segregation, can exist in any aspect of life, from housing, education, and employment to stores, recreational facilities, and other public places.

César quickly learned about the ugly realities of segregation.

Segregation that is allowed by law or some other government order is called de jure segregation. Segregation as a result of social factors is known as de facto segregation. When César Chávez was growing up, both de jure and de facto segregation existed in the United States.

Migrant families lived in makeshift labor camps like this one in Marysville, California, in the 1930s.

did not like being teased and harassed. "In integrated schools, where we were the only Mexicans, we were like monkeys in a cage," said César. "There were lots of racist remarks that still hurt my ears when I think of them."[3] César and his siblings were punished for speaking Spanish in school. Teachers rapped the children's knuckles with a ruler or hit them with a paddle. One of César's teachers hung a sign around his neck that read, "I am a clown; I speak Spanish."[4]

César did not enjoy going to school, largely because of this kind of treatment by fellow students and some of the teachers. Some years the Chávez family was so poor that César had no shoes to wear to school. When he showed up barefoot or just in socks, he was teased mercilessly. It hurt César deeply when others made fun of his accent or when he overheard other kids saying "dirty Mexicans."[5]

After school, all the Chávez children were expected to work to earn money for the family. César and his brother Richard did a number of odd jobs to help provide for their family. They sold newspapers, chopped wood for other people, collected empty bottles and pieces of tin, and cleaned up at the local theater and boxing ring. Empty bottles and tin could be sold to scrap yards for extra money. One day, the brothers sold a ball of tinfoil they had been making from discarded cigarette wrappers. César and Richard were thrilled when it weighed in at eighteen pounds. With the money they collected, the brothers were able to buy two sweatshirts and a pair of sneakers.[6]

The life of migrant workers was very harsh. While the Great Depression affected virtually everyone, migrant agricultural workers suffered greater hardships. A 1940 U.S. Senate report described farmworkers as "ill-fed, ill-clothed, poorly housed and almost completely lacking in many other things commonly considered necessary for civilized life."[7] Luciano Martínez, a farmworker in the Coachella Valley of California, later recalled having to "sneak [bites of] his lunch into his mouth because fieldworkers were not allowed to eat on the job."[8]

César and his family sometimes lived in migrant

Being a child of migrant farmworkers meant never truly having a home.

Like their parents, migrant children had to work all day long in the hot sun.

worker camps. Other times, they had no choice but to camp out under bridges and in shacks made out of cardboard and tar paper. César's sister Rita said, "We never lived away from our home. Here we come to California, and we were lucky we got a tent. Most of the time we were living under a tree, with just a canvas on top of us, and sometimes in the car."[9]

In 1939, the Chávez family settled for a time in a San Jose *barrio* (Latino neighborhood) that was called *Sal Si Puedes*, which means "Get Out If You Can." But getting out was only half the problem. The overcrowded area was made up of cramped shacks and old houses, unpaved streets, no sidewalks, no streetlights, and no sanitation system. César and the other members of his family had to live a single room in a lodging house.

After they left San Jose, the family moved on to Oxnard, where they picked walnuts until winter. During that cold winter, the family had no other place to stay than an eight-foot tent in an open field. Because it was close to the Pacific Ocean, a thick, damp fog kept their clothes and bedding perpetually cold and clammy. The tent was too small to fit the entire family, so César and his brothers Richard and Lenny slept outside. In the morning, the three boys would get dressed while they

Squatting for hours to pick fruits and vegetables can cause permanent back problems.

were still in their bedding. As soon as they jumped out, their feet would be covered with mud.[10]

Migrant farmworkers were paid very poorly. At one farm, César and his family were hired to pick peas. The youngest Chávez child, Lenny, had the job of keeping the family's water jug filled. They needed to drink lots of water in the hot sun. Working stooped over, César and the others had to pick very carefully. They would be paid only for produce that was considered good. At the end of three hours of backbreaking work, the entire family was paid only twenty cents.[11]

As meager as the income was when they worked, it was even worse when there were no crops to pick. During these especially hard times, the family did odd jobs for farmers and for other families.

The Chávez family had to be on the alert so they would not get cheated out of pay. Sometimes the bosses would rig the scales to show less weight than the workers actually picked. One time while waiting to get her sack weighed, César's mother caught the contractor cheating the worker in line in front of her. When Juana pointed it out, the contractor was so angry that he fired the entire Chávez family.

The growers also offered food items and goods for sale at the company store for double or triple the usual price. The workers, often without transportation and with no other place to shop, had no choice but to pay the high prices. César said, "We thought that always you

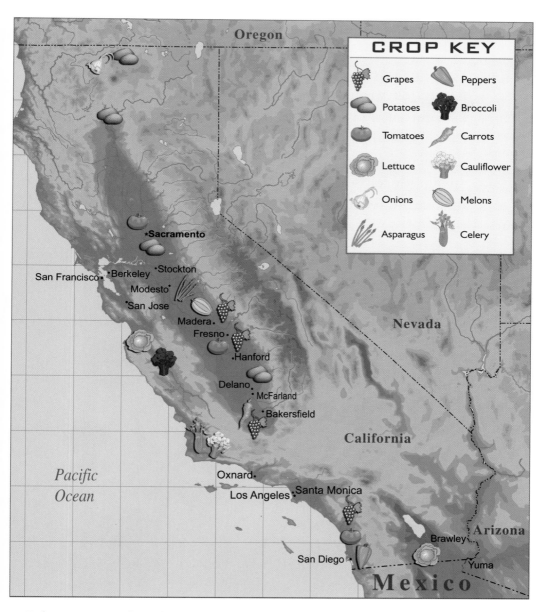

This map of California shows cities that were important in César's early life and later career. Symbols indicate some of the major areas producing crops picked by migrant workers.

had to suffer and be hungry. . . . That was our life."[12] It was a miserable way to live.

When one of the workers was mistreated, the Chávez family felt wronged, too. If someone quit because he had gotten shortchanged, the Chávez family quit also. César said that they were the first to leave the field if someone yelled "*¡Huelga!*" (Strike!). César recalled, "If any family felt something was wrong and stopped working, we immediately joined them even if we didn't know them."[13]

Young César poses with some of his siblings and friends on the family car.

During this time, a union representative paid Librado a visit. A labor union is an organization of workers formed to improve the welfare of its members. Labor unions deal with employers for better contracts, higher wages, and safer working conditions. The idea behind a labor union is that together the workers have a voice, while alone they are easily ignored

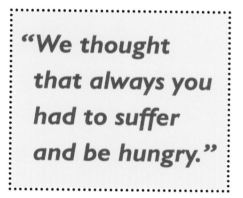

"We thought that always you had to suffer and be hungry."

or replaced. The man told Librado that by joining the union, Librado and his family would get better working conditions and maybe better pay. Because the Chávez family harvested so many different crops, Librado eventually joined several different unions, such as the Cannery Workers' Union, the Packing House Workers Union, and the Tobacco Workers' Union.

Many agricultural unions were swiftly crushed, however. When the workers went on strike, the growers would simply hire more farmworkers to break the strike. Still, Librado and others continued to join the unions. Little did Librado realize that he was providing a valuable lesson for young César—a lesson that would soon direct the course of his son's life.

César holds his diploma after graduating from eighth grade, which marked the end of his schooling. The family needed the fifty or sixty cents he could earn in the fields every day.

Finding His Way

In 1942, César's father was injured in a car accident. For one month, he was unable to work. Understanding his family's crisis, fifteen-year-old César dropped out of school to work full-time in the fields. He had graduated from eighth grade—a high achievement for a migrant child—and had planned to earn a high school diploma. But his family needed his help.

It was about this time that César met Helen Fabela. Helen was born on January 21, 1928, in Brawley, California. Her parents were from Mexico. Helen's family, like César's, had become migrant workers after the economic hardships brought on by the Great Depression. Helen's father had died while she was in high school. To help her widowed mother earn money to take care of the family, Helen left school to work full-time picking crops. Helen and César would see each other from time to time at the local soda shop.

César's days were spent in the fields. Along with his brother Richard, César began to take on more responsibility at home. He learned the harvest schedule of various crops and helped decide when and where the family would move next.

Still, in other ways César was a typical teenager, rebelling against his parents. He liked to dance and hang out with his friends. He started listening to the big band sound of Duke Ellington, rather than traditional Mexican mariachi music. He rejected his mother's folk remedies in favor of modern medicine. He also started dressing in the fashionable *pachuco* style of the day.

Pachucos, as the young Mexican-American men were called, styled their hair in a ducktail and wore baggy pants with long key chains, long coats with wide shoulders, thick-soled shoes, and wide, flat hats often sporting a flashy feather. Originally associated with African-American youth culture and jazz, the oversized

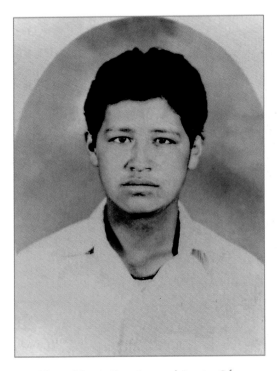

After his father's accident, César took over driving the family car and began making decisions for the family.

outfits were sometimes called zoot suits. Many people connected this style of clothing with gangs and violence, but others, including César, just liked the fashion. Like teenagers in every era, the *pachucos* wanted their own special look and identity.

In the 1940s, the *pachucos* were the targets of attacks known today as the Zoot Suit Riots or the Sailor Riots. In June 1943, a group of sailors on shore leave in Los Angeles claimed that a gang of *pachucos* had attacked them. The following night, a group of more than two hundred sailors in uniform stormed into a Mexican-American neighborhood in east Los Angeles. The sailors attacked anyone in a zoot suit. The servicemen tore off the *pachucos'* clothing, beat them, and left them in the streets. The assaults occurred for several more nights. The police did not stop the sailors, believing, like many in the community, that the beatings would halt an alleged "Mexican crime wave." Hundreds of Mexican-American youths were arrested without cause. The police said that the arrests were "preventive."[1] The military police finally stopped these assaults on the fifth night, when they forbade their servicemen from going to Los Angeles.

> Like teenagers everywhere, César had his own ideas about music and clothes.

Despite these disturbing reports about the military,

Seventeen-year-old César looked forward to better days in the navy, but he was sorely disappointed.

César joined the U.S. Navy in 1944, when he was seventeen. He was tired of farm work and thought that he might prefer being a sailor. Because the military was still segregated at that time, César was a deckhand, as were most enlisted Mexican Americans. The sailors who do manual labor on the ship, including cleaning and moving cargo, are called deckhands. César mostly worked as a painter while he was in the navy.

The navy did not turn out to be the escape that César had hoped for. He later described the two years he served as "the worst of my life."[2] He hated the strict chain of command, he disliked the food, and he was very disheartened by the discrimination he saw. During his days as a sailor, César once again felt the sting of racism.

One weekend César and two of his navy buddies were on a seventy-two-hour leave in Delano, California. The three decided to go to the movies. The only movie theater in town was segregated, with separate seating areas for whites and nonwhites. César decided that he would challenge the rule by sitting in an area reserved for white people. When he was asked to move to the section where Mexicans were allowed to sit, he refused. The police were called, and they took César to jail. The booking officer on duty did not know what to charge César with, because he was not drunk and was not disturbing the peace. After some questioning, César was released. It was the first time he had so openly stood up for his beliefs.

César left the navy in 1946. He rejoined his family in Delano and began working in the fields once more. When he met up again with Helen Fabela, they started dating and soon fell in love.

The two married on October 22, 1948. Helen was twenty; César was twenty-one. For their honeymoon, the newlyweds drove through California, visiting the missions that had been built by the Spanish many

César and Helen enjoyed being together for a movie or a walk along the ocean.

years before. César had saved some money, and they were able to borrow the family car. It was a rare luxury for them to vacation for two weeks.

Back in Delano, César found a job, and he and Helen moved into a one-room shack with no water or electricity. They had no car of their own, so getting places was very difficult. It was a challenging time for the couple. They soon learned that Helen was pregnant. Once their son Fernando was born, their lives became even harder.

Eventually, César and his brother Richard found jobs in a lumber mill and returned to San Jose, California. César and Helen found a small house in the dismal *Sal Si Puedes* and settled in with their growing family. Helen soon gave birth to a second child, Sylvia, and then a third, Linda. Together, the couple would raise eight children.

While living in *Sal Si Puedes*, Chávez met Father Donald McDonnell, a Catholic priest who held mass in a small meeting hall. Father McDonnell talked with Chávez about the conditions of farmworkers and began lending him some thought-provoking books. What Chávez did not know was that his education in labor organizing and civil rights had officially begun.

Organizing to Fight Injustice

César Chávez remembered the comforting lessons his grandmother, Mama Tella, had given him about their religion, Catholicism. At Father McDonnell's church, the priest's work inspired Chávez, and the two men began having conversations about all the difficulties faced by the migrant farmworkers.

Father McDonnell told Chávez about St. Francis of Assisi, a gentle and generous man known for his sympathy for the poor and unfortunate. Chávez was moved by the story and learned a great deal about the life of this saint. While reading a biography of the saint, he came across the name of Mahatma Gandhi.

Mahatma Gandhi was a leader in India who championed the rights of Indian citizens in their British-controlled country. He advocated peaceful civil disobedience and nonviolence. In large part because of Gandhi's efforts, Great Britain granted independence to India in 1947. When Chávez read *Gandhi: His Life and Message for the World*, the Indian leader's ideas and actions inspired him. Like Gandhi, Chávez believed that violence leads only to more violence. After reading Gandhi's autobiography, *The Story of My Experiments With Truth*, Chávez was ready to act.

Meanwhile, Father McDonnell had been in touch with Fred Ross, a national organizer for the Community Service Organization (CSO), a group fighting for civil rights. Several times Ross had asked to meet with Chávez, but Chávez had declined, suspicious of Anglos (white Americans) working on behalf of Mexican Americans. Ross persisted, and finally, in 1952, after Ross made several visits to the barrio where Chávez lived, Chávez agreed to hear what Ross had to say.

Ross's sincerity immediately impressed Chávez, who later said, "My suspicions were erased. . . . I saw [Ross] organize, and I wanted to learn."[1] Ross convinced Chávez that they were working for the same cause and asked him to join the CSO. Chávez agreed, and after a brief spell as a volunteer, he was officially hired by the CSO for $35 a week. Before long, Ross and Chávez had organized more than twenty CSO chapters.

Chávez was twenty-five years old when he joined the CSO. His alliance with Ross proved to be very valuable. In addition to becoming a lifelong friend, Ross taught Chávez effective organizing strategies. To rally support, Ross used an organizing method known as the house meeting approach.[2] This involved gathering people at one of the farmworkers' homes, where they would feel more comfortable. All the people attending would then be asked to host a meeting in *their* homes and to bring even more new people into the movement.

At first, Chávez was so nervous that he would get to a meeting early and then drive around the neighborhood, too shy to go in. Finally, he would gather his courage and force himself to go inside. Chávez was so young and slender that he would often go unnoticed. "Where's the organizer?" people would ask. When Chávez responded, "Here I am!" they would reply, "Ha! This *kid*?"[3] But Chávez soon won them over with his sincerity and tireless commitment to improving their work conditions.

As part of the Community Service Organization (CSO), Chávez worked day and night to encourage farmworkers to register to vote.

Ross also emphasized voter registration and voter education so that the workers could make good, informed decisions at the polls. Increasing the number of farmworkers who voted would increase their power in electing officials. Chávez was so effective at getting Mexican Americans registered to vote that he was soon assigned the complicated task of helping Mexican immigrants become United States citizens. In 1959 Chávez became the executive director of the CSO in California.

While working at the CSO, Chávez met Dolores Huerta, a Mexican-American woman with seemingly boundless energy and enthusiasm. Although she had

Here, Dolores Huerta was helping to register some voters.

never been a farmworker, she had helped her mother run a boardinghouse for migrant workers. Like Chávez, Huerta wanted to correct the injustices and miserable conditions that farmworkers endured.

Dolores Huerta had been working at the CSO for several months before she met Chávez. She later said, "It was at a meeting, and five minutes after I met him, I couldn't find him again. He looked like everybody else. He was not the kind of person who called attention to himself."[4]

Despite the good work that the CSO was doing, Chávez was not satisfied with the scope of its activities. The CSO's main focus was on urban Mexican Americans. While he knew that helping that population was certainly important, Chávez felt that farmworkers' rights were not being adequately represented. He was outraged that most of the farmworkers did not get rest breaks or have portable toilets or fresh water to drink in the fields. They were not entitled to health or medical insurance. And the methods used to work the fields required the workers to be stooped over for long hours at a time. It was no wonder that many of them called the crops they picked *la fruta del Diablo* (the fruit of the devil).[5]

There was no union to protect the workers or to negotiate on their behalf. One had existed in 1928—the Imperial Valley Workers' Union—but it had been defeated by the powerful growers. Later in the 1930s, rich growers shut down two other unions (the

Confederation of Mexican Farmworkers and the Cannery and Agricultural Workers' Industrial Union).

Agribusiness was—and still is—an important part of the California economy. Agribusiness is large-scale farming that includes the production, processing, and distribution of agricultural products. In addition to the growers, agribusiness also has the backing of banks, big investment corporations, and often the government. Unions that represent the workers are usually at odds with agribusiness.

Chávez felt ready to go beyond the work of the CSO. He wanted to take a stand and speak out for the farmworkers. By 1962 he was earning a steady paycheck of $150 per week at the CSO. The thirty-five-year-old father of eight wondered if he would be able to meet his family's needs without this stable job. His oldest child was thirteen and his youngest was two and a half. How would his wife, Helen, react when he told her his dreams? He should not have worried; Helen understood the importance of his plans. She said, "I'm willing to stick it out for ten years and really give it a trial. If it doesn't work, we can figure out something else."[6]

In 1962, at the CSO's annual convention, Chávez proposed creating a union for farmworkers. The board of directors declined, saying that the CSO was a civil rights organization, not a labor union. After ten years with the CSO, Chávez resigned from the organization and vowed to make his vision of a farmworkers' union a reality.

Helen and César Chávez, with six of their eight children.

One of the union workers later said, "Chávez wanted not just a decent wage. He wanted farmworkers, educated and uneducated, white, black and brown, to be accepted as human beings by their employers and to have the power to control their own lives."[7]

The same year that Chávez quit the CSO, Michael Harrington published his book *The Other America*. Describing in poignant detail the lives of the poor and downtrodden, Harrington's book opened many people's eyes to the crippling poverty that existed in the United States. Many Americans were shocked to learn that millions of people in the U.S.—many of them farmworkers—lived at levels "beneath those necessary for human decency," wrote Harrington.[8]

With Helen's support, César Chávez had decided he was ready to take the plunge. Using their life savings of $1,200, he set out to create a farmworkers' union. It was a decision that would prove to be immensely important for farmworkers everywhere.

La Causa Is Born

César Chávez could hardly believe his eyes. The hall in Fresno, California, was crowded with 150 delegates from union offices all over the state. Across the back of the stage was draped a bold flag: a black eagle in a white circle on a red background. Chávez had wanted a union logo that could be easily duplicated by the union members. The Mexican symbol of an eagle with a snake in its mouth was too difficult to draw. Chávez liked the suggestion of an eagle drawn with straight lines and sharp corners; it seemed a good solution. After reading that the ancient Egyptians had found the color combination of red, white, and black to be very striking, César chose those dramatic colors for the flag. The black stood for the dark situation facing farmworkers, the red background symbolized the sacrifices made by the workers, and the white circle represented hope.

In 1962, after resigning from the CSO, Chávez and

Chávez called the union logo "a strong, beautiful sign of hope."

his CSO colleagues Dolores Huerta and Gilbert Padilla established the National Farmworkers Association (NFWA). Soon Richard Chávez and cousin Manuel Chávez also joined them. Because they wanted to create an organization that really met the needs of its members, César Chávez traveled to many fields and camps to talk to workers, tell them about his idea for a farmworkers' union, and get their input for creating it. Meanwhile, his wife, Helen, worked in the fields to support their family.

César Chávez wanted to have a multicultural union. He believed that union membership and volunteers should be made up of many different types of people. He said that if there were only Mexican farmworkers in the union, there would be no new ideas. He said, "It's beautiful to work with other groups, other ideas, and other customs."[1]

House meetings were an effective way to spread the word and build loyalty. In an individual's home, people were less fearful than they would have been in the field with bosses looking on. Chávez passed out questionnaires and interviewed people to determine which services they needed most. He also believed, "Meetings have to be short and to the point. There is nothing more disastrous than to have meetings which ramble on and on without any results."[2]

Chávez insisted that the workers must help to build the union. He believed that workers themselves had to commit to, invest in, and have pride in the organization. He said, "I have always believed that in order for any movement to be lasting, it must be built on the people. They must be the ones involved in forming it, and they must be the ones that ultimately control it."[3]

One time, after observing Dolores Huerta investing so much energy on behalf of some of the workers, Chávez told her, "You are giving away your services to the workers, but you are not getting any commitments from them."[4] As Rita Chávez later explained, "The core idea of organizing was to get people to do for themselves, not to do it for them . . . they put the responsibility right

Huerta, Antonio Orendain, and Chávez at the first NFWA convention in 1962.

back to the workers. You want a union? O.K. then you got to build it."[5]

The first thing Chávez and his associates did was to reflect on what had not worked at the CSO. The most pressing challenge had been finances. At the CSO, yearly dues were $5. It became clear to Chávez, Huerta, and others that the union would have to raise funds. After much thought and debate, they decided to set the dues at $3.50 per month, or $42 per year. For poor farmworkers, the difference between $5 and $42 dollars a year was huge. Huerta later recalled asking, "How could we ever form a union when the workers were so poor they could hardly pay the necessary dues?"[6] But once they realized the many benefits they would get as a result of the union, the workers found ways to come up with their dues.

One benefit that was used to recruit members was burial and death insurance. Union membership guaranteed members the basic human right of being buried in a simple pine coffin and having a small amount of money granted to survivors. The union contracted with an insurance company so that in the event of death, the family would receive $1,000 for the head of the household and $500 for each dependent. Dolores Huerta explained, "Every time one of the workers died, we had a get-together, not only to pay our respects, but also to let everybody know that if they joined the United Farmworkers they would receive this little death benefit."[7]

Chávez used images familiar to Mexican Americans in his organizing. In addition to the union flag, images of the *Virgen de Guadalupe* were displayed at meetings and rallies. *La Virgen de Guadalupe* is the patron saint of Mexico. She has been a symbol of hope and protection since the sixteenth century and is still a powerful figure throughout Latin America. Dolores Huerta said that for the farmworkers, the Virgin was a "symbol of the impossible."[8] On the back of his old station wagon, Chávez created a shrine, using the Virgin, candles, flowers, and flags.

The NFWA also published a bilingual newspaper in Spanish and English called *El Malcriado*. The title literally means "the ill-bred child" and refers to children who misbehave or are spoiled. Chávez got the name from one of the papers popular during the Mexican Revolution. In addition to editorials and essays that called for the end of the farmworkers' exploitation, *El Malcriado* also included witty cartoons ridiculing the rich growers. The newspaper came out twice a month and sold out almost as fast as the NFWA staff could publish it.

From the beginning, women were an important part of *La Causa* ("The Cause," a name for the union movement). Jessie De La Cruz, one of the first women organizers, said that Chávez "was the first person to tell us that women were equal to men and that we had the same rights."[9] Dolores Huerta, cofounder of the NFWA, served as the union's first vice president. At that time, she was a single mother with seven children (she would eventually have eleven children). Huerta said, "Poor people's movements have always had whole families on the line, ready to move at a moment's notice, with more courage because that's all we had."[10]

At first, some people did not know how to deal with such a strong Latina in a leadership position. One grower, after meeting with her said, "Dolores Huerta is crazy. She is a violent woman, where women, especially Mexican women, are usually peaceful and calm."[11] Many of the men who had to negotiate with Huerta were not prepared for her commanding, passionate style.

As a mother, Huerta was also criticized for her nontraditional approach to raising a family. Because she was so heavily involved in union activities, she often had to make child-care arrangements. When she traveled, she sometimes had to leave her children for extended periods of time with family members. Huerta noted that it was mostly middle-class people who criticized her. She said the middle class was, "more hung-up about these things than the poor people are, because the poor people have to haul their kids around from school to school, and women have to go out and work and they've got to either leave their kids or take them out to the fields with them."[12]

Another woman vital to the union's efforts was Helen Chávez. Even though she shunned the limelight and did not hold an official position in the NFWA,

Chavez believed that women were equal to men and deserved the same rights.

Helen's behind-the-scenes work was crucial for the union's success. Often she would work late at night, after her household chores were done and the children were put to bed. "If we were going to have a meeting," she said, "I would address all the envelopes or address post cards, whatever had to be done."[13] Eventually, Helen became the bookkeeper of the union's credit union bank. She served in that capacity for more than twenty years.

Like his role model Mahatma Gandhi, César Chávez lived simply, to the point of self-denial. The house in

Credit Unions

Credit unions offer another way for working people to control their own lives, rather than giving that control to big business. A credit union is a bank that is owned by the people who deposit money there, not by stockholders. Credit unions, like banks, safeguard depositors' money and make loans to their members. But unlike other banks, credit unions do not operate for profit. This keeps operating costs lower than for other financial institutions. As a result, members can get loans at lower rates at their credit union than they can at other banks.

Credit unions may be organized by depositor occupation, community, church group, or other type of "union." The first credit union in the United States was established in Massachusetts in 1909.

which he, Helen, and their eight children lived had only two bedrooms, a living room, and a kitchen. Former California governor and personal friend Jerry Brown said that Chávez set an example by his frugal and sharing ways: "He went against the grain by living simply despite his fame."[14] Chávez wore simple clothing, as a workingman would. Most often, he wore khaki pants, flannel shirts, or *guayaberas*—short-sleeved shirts popular in Latin America. He did not use fancy products like cologne, aftershave lotion, or hair tonics.[15]

Over the course of his life, Chávez never owned a home or any land. When the union was first started,

NFWA workers were paid $10 a week. Because the union did not have much in the treasury, Chávez would keep just $5 of his weekly salary and donate $5 back to the union.[16] He never made more than $6,000 a year in his entire life.

From reading about Gandhi, Chávez had learned about nonviolent strategies of civil disobedience such as strikes, picket lines, boycotts, marches, demonstrations, and fasts. He decided that these strategies could also be effective for the NFWA. Dolores Huerta once

Helen Chávez was a tremendous help to *La Causa*.

53

described the power of nonviolence, saying, "It eventually touches the people that are perpetuating the violence. It touches them. I've seen that happen a lot."[17]

Chávez explained why Gandhi became one of his role models:

> The message for me is that of his nonviolence and the fact that he was a doer. He made things happen. I lose faith in someone who doesn't continue a project, who starts something and then leaves it. The world is full of us quitters. Even if Gandhi had not liberated India, he stayed with the project all his life. And that is my great attraction. He just didn't give up.[18]

One of the first tactics the NFWA used was staging a strike. When employees go on strike, it means that they have agreed that the whole group will stop working as a way to protest their employer's unfair practices. While they are on strike, the workers often also have a picket line. The picketers hold up signs expressing their discontent.

Although the NFWA picketers were often treated badly, Chávez was strict about the union's conduct while they were on strike. Strikers could not block traffic, could not litter, could not use foul language, and could not return insults.[19] Chávez insisted that the striking workers conduct themselves in such a way that they could not possibly be criticized for their protest.

Although it was sometimes very difficult to stay peaceful, Chávez held fast to his belief in nonviolence. He told union members, "People don't like to see a nonviolent movement subjected to violence, and there's a lot of support across the country for nonviolence. That's the key point we have going for us. We can turn the world if we can do it nonviolently."[20]

Although Chávez was soft-spoken, many people were drawn to his quiet charisma. One former aide said, "When [Chávez] talked to you, he let you know that you were the whole world for him."[21] Chávez took the name of the barrio *Sal Si Puedes* and reordered the words into "*¡Sí, Se Puede!*" (Yes, It Can Be Done!). One supporter of the union said, "César was not an electrifying public speaker—yet he commanded attention and respect and people remembered his message."[22]

Chávez's simple way of speaking was very effective. At a rally for grape workers, he told a story about a man with a whip. The man was so precise with his whip that he could flick the ashes off a man's cigarette while it was being smoked. Because of his temper and his skill with the whip, people were afraid of him. One day a bee buzzed by his head and would not go away when he tried to brush it away with his hand. One of the man's workers noticed what was happening and expressed his surprise, asking why the man did not use his whip on the bee. The man answered that although he could kill the bee, it was different from other things he had

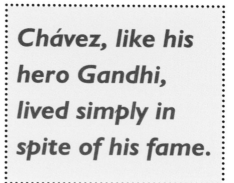

Chávez, like his hero Gandhi, lived simply in spite of his fame.

whipped before. "If you go after one," he said, "they all come after you."

Chávez paused dramatically, then said, "That is what the union means. The union is like the bees, and the man with the whip is like the grower. He cannot do anything to one of us without having all of us come after him."[23] As Chávez's words sank in, the crowd erupted into cheers.

Chávez's religion also inspired him. Chávez, a devout Catholic, attended church services regularly. He once said, "To me, religion is a most beautiful thing. . . . I have come to realize that all religions are beautiful. Your religion just happens to depend a lot on your upbringing and your culture."[24] Many of his union protests started and ended with a Catholic mass. Years later, he was able to make a lifelong dream of meeting the pope come true. Chávez, his wife, Helen, and a son-in-law traveled to Europe as part of an effort to educate Europeans about the mistreatment of farmworkers in the United States. Chávez refused to accept union funds for the trip, but several other organizations contributed money. While there, in a visit that Chávez called a "small miracle," he and Helen were able to meet Pope Paul VI.[25]

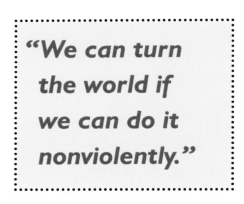

"We can turn the world if we can do it nonviolently."

Sometimes Chávez would quote Bible passages to underscore his message. One time, as he was sharing his vision of a day when migrant workers would get their due, he said:

> That day may not come this year. That day may not come during this decade. But it will come, someday! And when that day comes, we shall see the fulfillment of that passage from the Book of Matthew in the New Testament, "That the last shall be first and the first shall be last."[26]

All of Chávez's strategies and hard work paid off. By 1965, the union had nearly two thousand members. The credit union had more than $25,000. That same year, Chávez learned that Filipino grape workers in California were on strike. The Filipino union called upon Chávez and the NFWA to join them in striking against some of the most powerful growers. Chávez certainly believed in their cause, but was his young union ready for such a big fight?

¡Huelga!

The strike had started when Filipino-American grape pickers in Delano, California, walked off the job. They were tired of toiling long hours in the fields for wages that were under the poverty level. They each made about $2,400 per year.[1] At the time, even $3,223 was not considered enough for a family of four to live on.

After the grape pickers appealed for help, Chávez called for a meeting of the union on September 16, 1965, Independence Day in Mexico. He and others took turns speaking to the NFWA members in attendance and asking for their support. When the union members voted, they overwhelmingly supported the strike. Chávez begged everyone to remain peaceful even if violence was used against them. According to Dolores Huerta, Chávez "was convinced that if we resorted to violence, people would start killing each other and the killing would never end."[2]

Religious pictures hung alongside the union posters on Chávez's office wall.

Over the next few days, more than twelve hundred Mexican farmworkers walked off the fields. The strike was the largest in California history. It affected thousands of workers and covered an area of 450 square miles. Many of the union members, although supporting the strike, were unable to pay their dues. Other labor organizations—the AFL-CIO being the most notable—made contributions to keep the NFWA afloat financially.

Many of the strikers lived in labor camps on land owned by the growers that hired them. To retaliate against the strikers, some of the growers cut off the gas, water, and electricity at the camps. At some camps, when the workers returned to their modest homes at the end of the day, they found their meager belongings thrown in the dirt near the fields.

When there was a strike, NFWA workers and volunteers would set up a picket line alongside a field where scabs (strikebreakers) were working. The growers hired private security officers to patrol the picket line near their fields. The picketers would shout to the workers, asking them to join them on the line. The hired security would shout, too, so the workers would not be able hear the picketers' invitation. Sometimes the growers played music over loudspeakers to drown out the picketers' voices.[3]

The NFWA picketers held fast to their goal of nonviolence. But it was hard when they were tripped, elbowed, or pushed by the growers' hired security guards or police. One of the tactics the growers used was driving a tractor close to the picket line and covering the picketers with dirt. One grower even sprayed the picketers with sulfur, a dangerous chemical. Although he was later taken to court for this action, the grower was acquitted.[4]

Sadly, one of the Filipino picketers, Paulo Agbayani, suffered heatstroke and a heart attack in the hot California sun. He later died. The legs of another striker, Manuel Rivera, were crushed when a car ran through a picket line. The clashes turned even more deadly when growers started to equip their foremen and security guards with clubs and guns.

> *Chávez urged the strikers to keep their protest peaceful —even in the face of violence.*

One of the biggest challenges for the NFWA was trying to persuade the *esquiroles* (strikebreakers) to leave the fields and join the strike. Desperate for a day's pay, many people went past the picketers to work in the fields. With their grapes rotting on the vines, the growers sometimes resorted to sending children out to do the work.

As the strike wore on, Chávez realized that a strike alone was not enough. He remembered the salt boycott led by Mahatma Gandhi in India. Gandhi had showed

People picketed outside grocery stores.

how an unjust law could be challenged peacefully. With a boycott, consumers completely stop buying a product in order to force a change in policy or pricing. The people of India had become fed up with the high tax that the British government put on salt. Gandhi called for a boycott. No one bought any salt, and the British soon backed down.

Chávez and the other union workers had also seen how effective the 1955 bus boycott in Montgomery, Alabama, had been for the American civil rights movement.

The Power of Nonviolent Protest

The boycott of buses in Montgomery, Alabama, was led by the Reverend Martin Luther King, Jr., another important role model for Chávez. Dr. King, too, modeled his actions on the example of nonviolent protest set by Mahatma Gandhi. It was the bus boycott that first propelled King into the national spotlight.

Martin Luther King, Jr., also admired and learned from Mahatma Gandhi.

The boycott began in December 1955 after Rosa Parks, an African-American seamstress, was arrested for refusing to give up her seat to a white man on a city bus. At the time, African Americans had to sit in the back on public buses, and they had to yield their seats if there was not enough room in the front for all the white people. The African Americans of Montgomery rallied to fight the segregation laws through the courts. They also applied pressure on the bus company by boycotting the buses. They stayed off the buses for a full year. In 1956 the U.S. Supreme Court ruled that segregated seating on buses was unconstitutional. The Montgomery bus boycott is considered a milestone in the civil rights movement. It is also a testament to the power of nonviolent protest.

Chávez called for Americans to boycott table grapes. If enough people stopped buying grapes, then the growers would lose money. The NFWA hoped that when growers lost income, they would have no choice but to negotiate with the union. To publicize the boycott, union workers followed the grape-delivery trucks to the markets. There, in front of the grocery stores, the unions set up picket lines and distributed pamphlets to shoppers. Sometimes the strike supporters gave children helium-filled balloons stamped BOYCOTT GRAPES.

People young and old pitched in to help with the strike and the boycott.

As shoppers learned of the unfair working conditions, many of them joined the boycott, refusing to buy the grapes.

NFWA volunteers thoroughly covered an area by dividing it into sections. The union worker responsible for each section took charge of contacting local organizations, distributing printed leaflets to consumers, and picking up support. "People want to help, the American public wants to help, they just have to know what to do. You have to give them a way that they can do it," said Dolores Huerta.[5] The NFWA persuaded many more consumers to boycott grapes.

Chávez also used the news media to publicize the boycott. He spoke at rallies and college campuses, called newspapers, and gave interviews to news reporters. He and the NFWA were also featured in a television show, *Harvest of Shame*. The documentary described the terrible conditions of U.S. migrant farmworkers. People across the nation learned of the unfair system that trapped migrant farmworkers.

About this time, the Federal Bureau of Investigation (FBI) started monitoring Chávez's activities. Some people charged that he might have Communist ties or that he might be involved in rebellious activities against the government. Others said that he might have taken money from the union treasury. After years of observation, it was finally concluded that there was no evidence to support any of the claims. In the end, the fifteen-hundred-page file that the FBI compiled just proved, as an FBI informant later said, that Chávez "was among this country's few great selfless mass leaders."[6]

Of the many papers in the FBI file are documents pointing to the agency's discomfort with the word *huelga* (strike). Some in the FBI wondered if the word had a larger meaning. Indeed, the Kern County sheriff's department issued an order prohibiting local strikers from using the word. The NFWA sent a group of fourty-four strikers, including Helen Chávez, to a Delano ranch and instructed them to shout "*¡Huelga!*" as they took their places on the picket line. The officers on duty promptly arrested the whole group, including Helen. Her words reflected the feelings of those arrested for *La Causa*: "Being in jail didn't scare me because I know that what I'm doing is right and that I'm doing it for people who have worked and sacrificed so hard."[7] She and others spent three days in jail. Meanwhile, hundreds of supporters gathered outside, singing protest songs and calling media attention to this injustice.

The Chávezes' work was not always easy on their children. César was often absent for long periods of time. The children worried when their father or mother went out on picket lines, not knowing whether they would be arrested or beaten. They were teased in school. Fernando, the eldest son, was sent to live with his grandparents in another city to finish high school because of the many fights boys picked with him in school. Despite these difficulties, the children were proud of their parents and the important work they were doing.

In early 1966, Chávez began organizing a 340-mile march from Delano to Sacramento, the capital of California. He hoped that the march would bring even more attention to the strike and would also inspire new members to join. The march was planned to start on March 17 and to end on Easter Sunday. Because it would be during the Lenten season, Chávez called it a *peregrinación*, or pilgrimage. A pilgrimage is a long journey usually taken for a moral or spiritual purpose.

Striking grape pickers marched through California to gather support.

Lent refers to the forty-day period before the Christian holiday of Easter. It is a solemn time marked by fasting and penitence.

As the procession worked its way through the small towns, hundreds of people would greet the marchers and sometimes join them, helping them carry the flags to the next town. The march eventually took twenty-five days. Lalo Guerrero, a Latino musician, immortalized the march by writing a *corrido*, or folk ballad, called "El Corrido de Delano."

A theater troupe called El Teatro Campesino (The Farmworkers Theater) performed on its movable stage—a flatbed truck. The shows featured farmworkers doing improvised skits. The troupe had been started by Luis Valdez, a young theater director and actor who wanted to help Chávez spread the word about the grape boycott and raise money for his cause. When Valdez had first explained his idea to Chávez, the union leader said: "'There is no money, no actors. Nothing. Just workers on strike.'

"But he also told me that if I could put something together, it was OK with him. And that was all we needed—a chance. We jumped on top of a truck and started performing. Then something great happened. Our work raised the spirits of everyone on the picket lines and César saw that."[8] Using simple props, masks, and signs, El Teatro Campesino created skits that spoofed the growers and educated people about important issues.

Even pain and sickness could not stop Chávez from completing the march.

The march was very difficult. After just the first day, the marchers' feet were covered with painful blisters. One marcher said, "Some people had bloody feet. Some would keep on walking and you'd see blood coming out of their shoes."[9] One of Chávez's legs swelled, and he developed a high fever. Despite the severe pain, he refused medication and continued on the march, using a cane to help him walk.

Each night when the marchers stopped, they held a meeting to rally support and to educate the public. Hundreds of families hosted the marchers in each town, offering them a meal, a shower, and a bed so they could sleep before the next day's walk.

When the march ended on Easter Sunday, as planned, about ten thousand people joined Chávez and the marchers on the steps of the capitol. Martin Luther King, Jr., sent Chávez a telegram. In it, Dr. King sent his best wishes to Chávez and the union, saying: "Our separate struggles are really one—a struggle for freedom, for dignity, and for humanity. . . . We are together with you in spirit and in determination that our dreams for a better tomorrow will be realized."[10]

In August 1966, the NFWA and the Filipinos' union, the Agricultural Workers' Organizing Committee (AWOC), merged together and joined the larger AFL-CIO. Dolores Huerta said the merger was a matter of survival:

Umbrella Organizations: The AFL-CIO

Unions represent people in a particular occupation, such as farmworkers, steelworkers, miners, teachers, or truck drivers. In 1886, one of the first union networks, the American Federation of Labor (AFL), was founded. This federation helped people organize new unions and used the power of multiple unions to bargain for better working conditions. In 1938, some members of the AFL split off to create the Congress of Industrial Organizations (CIO). This faction welcomed unions that were not categorized by craft, but rather by industry. The two networks recombined in 1955, making the AFL-CIO. Four years later, the AFL-CIO would try to help the farmworkers organize a union.

By 2005, the AFL-CIO's network encompassed over sixty unions. Another umbrella organization for unions is the International Brotherhood of Teamsters, which was originally a union for people who drove teams of oxen.

Supporters of AFL-CIO leader Chávez celebrated his election victory over the rival Teamsters Union.

"Had we not merged, the Teamsters Union [a rival union favored by the growers] would have wiped us out."[11] The new name for the farmworkers union was the United Farmworkers of America (UFWA), which was eventually shortened to the United Farmworkers (UFW). This was an important development, because the much larger union could provide members with emergency financial assistance when there was a strike. The support and financial assistance of the AFL-CIO also led to the construction of the UFW headquarters called Forty Acres (Cuarenta Acres), where Chávez would stage his dramatic 1968 fast.

Although a few of the growers agreed to some wage increases and some health-care benefits, the bulk of the powerful grape growers refused to negotiate. But as Chávez pointed out, "Time accomplishes for the poor what money does for the rich."[12] But how much longer could he—or the farmworkers—wait?

Opposition

Not long after Chávez's historic fast, some terrible news rocked the nation. In April 1968, the great civil rights leader Martin Luther King, Jr., was assassinated. Along with many others, Chávez was devastated when he heard the news. King's civil rights work had been an inspiration and a guide for Chávez. King's death sent a current of shock throughout the union. Just two months later, Chávez became despondent when he learned of another leader's assassination.

Robert Kennedy had been a UFW supporter since its beginning. He had also become a friend of Chávez's and had been at his side when he broke his fast in March. When Robert Kennedy announced that he would run for president of the United States, the union rallied around him, gathering support and helping him campaign for the California primary. On June 5, 1968, Chávez was at the Ambassador Hotel in Los Angeles, where the victory party was to be held on the night of the primary election. He had arranged for a mariachi band to play in celebration. That night, Robert Kennedy was fatally shot; he died the next day.

Around the same time, the union began receiving threats against Chávez's life. The executive board voted to hire security guards for Chávez. He accepted, but true to his conviction of nonviolence, Chávez refused to allow the bodyguards to carry guns.

Chávez acquired two German shepherd guard dogs that he named Huelga and Boycott. Chávez became very close to the dogs and was convinced that negotiations went more smoothly when Boycott was present. At one of the union meetings, Chávez asked that Boycott be officially declared a negotiating consultant. Looking down at the dog, Chávez said, "Every time we take him we get good luck. Right, Boycott?" The dog jumped up and put his paws on the podium. The board unanimously voted to include Boycott.[1]

To put even more pressure on the growers, in 1969 Chávez extended the boycott to include all table grapes from California. Union members and volunteers throughout the United States picketed supermarkets and handed out literature informing consumers of the boycott. Before long, shipments of California grapes were virtually stopped to large cities such as Boston, Chicago, New York, and Philadelphia.[2] The public had responded to the union's campaign. Seventeen million consumers stopped buying grapes. The grape growers

Guard dogs Huelga and Boycott took good care of their master and brought Chávez luck, too.

were furious with Chávez. They filed a lawsuit against the union, saying that they had lost more than $25 million as a direct result of the boycott.

Chávez realized that it was not just the growers who opposed him and who took advantage of migrant workers. "Everything is interwoven with agribusiness," Chávez said. "When you take on the growers, you're also taking on the large insurance companies who also happen to be owners of land, and you're taking on the large banks, and the railroads, and the pesticide and fertilizer companies. Talk about a power base against

The grape boycott went national. Here, Chávez led picketers outside a supermarket in Seattle, Washington.

you!"[3] But Chávez remained unfazed, saying, "They've got the money. We've got the people."[4]

Finally, in 1970, the grape growers agreed to sign union contracts. On July 29, 1970, twenty-nine grape growers came to Forty Acres. On that historic day, they signed a contract that increased wages to $1.80 per hour (the national minimum wage was then $1.45 per hour). The growers also agreed to contribute ten cents per hour to the Robert Kennedy Health and Welfare Fund for the workers.

Chávez, in honor of the brave Filipino-American workers who first walked out in 1965, wore a traditional white Filipino shirt for the occasion. Remembering their sacrifices, Chávez said, "Ninety-five percent of the [Delano grape] strikers lost their homes and cars. But in losing those worldly possessions, they found themselves."[5]

Unfortunately, some of the worst violence the union had experienced spoiled the celebratory mood. On August 25, 1970, Jerry Cohen, an attorney for the union, went to a packing company to check on workers who were planning a sit-down strike. The owner refused Cohen's request to see the workers. As he turned to go, burly men hired by the company attacked Cohen from behind. After he was knocked down, one of the men punched Cohen in the head. A college volunteer who had accompanied Cohen was also knocked down, punched, and kicked. Ambulances arrived later and took the injured men to the hospital. Cohen suffered a concussion and had to be hospitalized for a week.

Later that year, on December 5, 1970, Chávez had to appear before a judge. He had disobeyed an earlier court order to suspend boycotts against two companies, Bud Antle Produce (a grower) and Dow Chemical Company. The judge fined the union $10,000. (This amount was later dropped to $1,000 after the union's lawyer pointed out to the judge that the higher sum was against the law.) The judge also ordered Chávez to jail, where he would have to stay until he lifted the boycotts

César Chávez is seen here signing the contract that ended the long grape strike.

against Bud Antle and Dow. Chávez refused to end the boycotts and grimly went to jail, not knowing how long he would be there.

Chávez was placed in solitary confinement so he would have no contact with any other prisoners. He soon worked out a schedule for himself, to avoid becoming overly frustrated or depressed. He set a time to exercise, a time to read, a time to meditate, and a time to sleep. He made sure he also had time to read and answer his mail. He received so many letters that it took three or four hours each day to read them all. Chávez later said, "A lot of the letters I received almost had tears in them, exclaiming how unfair it was."[6]

Meanwhile, outside the jail, Chávez's supporters maintained a vigil. A makeshift shrine with the Virgin of Guadalupe was set up on the back of a pickup truck. Chávez was visited by well-known people such as Coretta Scott King, Ethel Kennedy, and Bishop Patrick Flores. After Chávez had served twenty days in jail, the

California Supreme Court ordered his release. The Court also later ruled that the union did have the right to boycott.

At its peak in the 1970s, the UFW had nearly 100,000 members. Chávez worked hard to create a full-service union that provided benefits such as health care, education, financial assistance, and legal services. In 1971, the union headquarters were moved from Delano to a compound in the Tehachapi Mountains, 125 miles northeast of Los Angeles. The site had once been a tuberculosis sanitarium. The new headquarters was soon named La Paz (peace).

Some saw the moving of the headquarters as a sign that Chávez was becoming increasingly distant and inaccessible.[7] Conservative politicians and growers were not the only ones who opposed Chávez. Discontent started to develop within the union ranks, too. No doubt the long work hours and small salaries were starting to take their toll. Union organizers worked fifty-three-hour weeks, with overtime being the norm. High-level union organizers lived in meager quarters on the union compound. Each received a very small weekly sum for groceries. One staffer explained that for Chávez, "it was unthinkable that representatives of the poor be better off than those for whom they labor. . . . As a result, the union was staffed only by those with a strong and sincere interest in social justice."[8]

Some people criticized Chávez's methods and leadership style, saying that he was becoming too controlling.

Philip Vera Cruz, who had served as vice president of the union, later criticized Chávez, saying: "He was incapable of sharing power."[9] Opponents said he did not trust others to do the work and got caught up in too many details. Some complained that Chávez's management style was too hands-on, meaning that he wanted to be kept informed of details and participated in most of the decision-making. Others complained that the UFW executive board was appointing the organizers in the local union offices, rather than having them elected by the workers.

> No leader is ever free from controversy. Some people criticized Chávez as being too controlling.

Even people who admired him admitted that Chávez was sometimes difficult and could be too demanding. Dolores Huerta said, "César is both a strong leader and a taskmaster. He is terrible to work with. He is at work at five-thirty or six o'clock in the morning . . . he works on into the evening. He works Saturdays and Sundays. On one occasion, César wanted to have a meeting on New Year's Day, when everybody else had partied the night before."[10]

Bob and Liz Maxwell, who worked for the UFW, noted how hard Chávez worked. They said, "He was often at his office at 3:00 A.M. to read correspondence and dictate replies before the staff arrived. He worked intently all day, rarely napping in the afternoon. He traveled an enormous amount, visiting various union offices or flying across the country to speaking engagements and rallies."[11]

Chávez read voraciously, constantly learning and growing. A former UFW worker, Peter Velasco, said that Chávez was always well prepared for staff meetings. One day, Velasco commented on the number of new books that Chávez had in his office. Chávez replied, "Peter, if you don't read new books, you are left behind. I spend time reading into the night. I want to be ahead of others."[12]

Some criticized the UFW for patrolling the border between Arizona and Mexico to prevent undocumented workers from entering. One of the tactics that the growers used was hiring undocumented workers from Mexico as strikebreakers. New immigrants are often willing to work for less than the minimum wage. These laborers, desperate for work, would often break the UFW strikes.[13] Chávez tried to educate the new, incoming Mexican workers about the labor conditions and he would try to get them to join the strike. However, some people criticized him, saying he took things too far: singing in front of the strikebreakers' homes, parading up and down their streets, and even putting up signs that said A SCAB LIVES HERE.

Still others were suspicious of the UFW's use of a controversial group therapy technique, called The Game.

These people were caught after sneaking across the border from Mexico into the United States.

The intense group counseling strategy was developed by Synanon, a group that had gained notoriety for helping drug addicts kick their habit. Participants in The Game aggressively criticized each other, trying to expose fears and prejudices. The Game had only two rules: no physical violence and no leaving the session. Chávez had thought that it might help build morale in the union leadership. Instead, some of the union leaders left the UFW, saying that The Game was too competitive and promoted bad feelings among the staff.[14]

Chávez shrugged off these criticisms saying, "Working for a just world sometimes means speaking truth not only to power, but to our friends. Working for a just world sometimes means being labeled as a trouble-maker, a zealot or as unpatriotic or un-Christian."[15] A former staff member said that although they all worked long, hard hours, they "always kept sight of the fact that no matter how tough the union work seemed at times, the workers in the field had it much worse."[16]

While there were discontented staff members, many union workers described the atmosphere at the La Paz headquarters as being family-like. On some Saturdays, Chávez would set up a softball game (in which he served as pitcher) and then have a huge barbecue afterward. Easter and Christmas were celebrated with festive gatherings. La Paz also provided Chávez and his assistants with a place to retreat from the harsh glare of the media.

In 1971 the Arizona legislature passed a controversial farm labor law forbidding boycotts and strikes during harvest season. The law had been signed by the Republican governor, John R. "Jack" Williams. Chávez called for the repeal of the law as well as the recall of the governor. To bring attention to the issue, Chávez embarked on a fast, which he conducted in a Latino neighborhood in Phoenix. The fast was called off after twenty-four days when doctors noticed that Chávez had developed an irregular heartbeat. While the UFW did not achieve its goal of repealing the law or recalling the governor, thousands of Latinos were registered to vote. In the next election, their voices would be heard.

In the fall of 1972, the California legislature introduced a similar antiboycott law, Proposition 22. Powerful growers sponsored Proposition 22. This proposal sought to ban boycotting and to bar seasonal (migrant) workers from voting in elections. The UFW widely publicized the threat to workers that the law would cause and embarked on a voter-registration drive to defeat the measure. When voters went to the polls, they decisively rejected the proposition. Chávez proved that the UFW had strong support from its members and the public.

As the UFW grew more powerful and garnered more support, the number of skirmishes with growers and local law enforcement increased. During the summer of 1973—called a "bloody summer"—more than three thousand UFW members were arrested in Kern County, California. Hundreds of protesters were beaten, dozens were shot, and two were killed.

Nagi Daifullah, a twenty-four-year-old picketer, was hit with a policeman's flashlight. After he fell down, the officer dragged him, bumping Daifullah's head against the hard pavement. The next day, Daifullah died. When the case was later brought to trial, the officer was acquitted.

Just two days after Daifullah died, Juan de la Cruz

was shot in the chest while standing in a union picket line. The shot had come from a speeding car. De la Cruz died just a few hours later. When the shooter was apprehended, he defended himself by saying that he had feared for his life because the picketers were throwing rocks at him. He was acquitted of the crime.

Devastated by the news of these violent incidents, Chávez called off all picketing. Luis Valdez said that Chávez "felt personally responsible—I mean that in every sense of the word—personally responsible for the life and death of people in the union. And he didn't feel it was worth it."[17] Chávez started thinking about other strategies the UFW could use. He realized that farmworkers needed a farm labor law to protect them.

At a news conference in Miami, Florida, Chávez spoke to reporters about citrus-fruit workers.

The year 1975 became a historic one for farmworkers. In May the California legislature, with the support of Governor Jerry Brown, passed the California Agricultural Labor Relations Act, the first of its kind in the continental United States. Until that year, even when workers signed cards saying that they wanted to be represented by the UFW, the growers simply refused to let them. The new law affirmed the right to boycott, allowed migrant workers to vote, and compelled the growers to bargain with the union. It also required growers to give rest breaks to the workers and to provide toilets and fresh water in the fields. It proved to be a milestone in the history of workers' rights.

Another victory that year was the abolition of the short-handled hoe, called *el cortito* in Spanish. The short handle of the tool forced workers to toil in a bent-over position for many hours on end, causing great pain and sometimes permanent disability. Chávez himself had used one and remembered the back pain he had felt. In fact, Chávez suffered severe back pain most of his life. Workers rejoiced when the use of the tool was outlawed.

Just one month after the California Agricultural Labor Relations Act was passed, Chávez led a thousand-mile march from the Mexican border to Sacramento. The march took fifty-nine days to complete and ended at UFW headquarters. Along the way, the marchers held rallies, talked to *campesinos* (farmworkers), and held meetings to plan their strategy.

Despite the passage of the California Agricultural Labor Relations Act, the UFW was still having problems reaching the workers in the fields. When UFW organizers came to the fields to speak to the farmworkers, the growers posted guards at the entrances to prevent them

Use of the short-handled hoe was finally banned in 1975.

from coming in. The growers also hired expensive, skilled lawyers who diverted the UFW's attention and funds with legal battles.

In response, the UFW launched a legislative campaign that came to be known as Proposition 14. The initiative called for unlimited access to farmworkers by the union. Jerry Brown and President Jimmy Carter supported the measure. Landowners and oil companies mounted a countercampaign, claiming that Proposition 14 would threaten individuals' property rights. When it went to the ballot in November 1976, voters rejected the measure.

"We can turn the world if we can do it nonviolently," said Chávez.

The defeat of Proposition 14 greatly disappointed Chávez. As he reflected on what the union could have done differently, he decided it was time to reorganize and modernize the union. A new computer system was put in, and all records were computerized. He brought in management expert Kenneth Blanchard (author of *The One Minute Manager*) to lead a seminar for leaders in the union. Blanchard waived his usual fee and gave the seminar for free.

In 1979 the UFW would face one of its biggest challenges yet. The Imperial Valley lettuce strike affected nearly five thousand workers. The field workers strongly supported the strike and the majority of them joined the picket lines, refusing to pick the crops. The strong show of support greatly pleased Chávez. The elation would not last long, however. On February 10, twenty-seven-year-old Rufino Contreras led a group of UFW strikers onto an Imperial Valley lettuce field to speak with strikebreakers. Security guards hired by the grower fired shots; one of the bullets hit Contreras in the face, killing him immediately. When the case went to court, the charges were dismissed against Contreras's accused murderers because of lack of evidence.

Later Years

The twentieth anniversary of the UFW, in 1982, was celebrated with a party at Sacred Heart Catholic Church in San Jose, California. In the church auditorium, hundreds of workers, union members, and supporters came together to mark the occasion. Chávez said, "There is no life apart from the union. If the union falls apart when I am gone, I will have been a miserable failure."[1]

Later that year, helped by $1 million in campaign contributions from the growers, Republican George Deukmejian was elected governor of California. When he took office in 1983, Deukmejian began making it more difficult for the union to enforce the state's historic farm labor law. Thousands of farmworkers lost their UFW contracts. Growers fired many workers, then blacklisted them—that is, prevented them from getting hired elsewhere.

In addition to the ongoing labor problems, Chávez

became increasingly concerned about the use of pesticides. In the 1980s it was reported that U.S. farmers were using about 2.6 million tons of pesticides a year on their crops.[2] As commercial growers began to use more and more chemicals, Chávez concentrated his efforts on informing the public about the dangers of using pesticides and herbicides. Although no long-term studies had yet been done on these substances' effects, he believed that these chemicals were dangerous for consumers.

In addition to proposing that health problems for consumers were associated with pesticide residue on produce, Chávez also brought attention to the workers

Chávez was growing more worried about the poisonous pesticides that farmers were spraying on their crops.

who were sprayed while they were working in the fields. Many workers experienced rashes, peeling skin, stomachaches, vomiting, and red and swollen eyes. Some had their vision impaired, became unconscious, or even died.[3] Worrisome rates of cancer, especially among children, were also reported. Chávez was enraged when he learned that a laborer had become ill after working in a recently sprayed field. The grower decided to drive him to a clinic across the U.S.-Mexico border, about an hour away. The farmworker never made it; he died on the way.

To educate the public about the widespread use of chemicals on produce, Chávez launched a new boycott of table grapes in June 1984. It was not as effective as the union would have hoped. To help spread the word, the union produced *The Wrath of Grapes*, a sixteen-minute movie that graphically illustrated the effects of pesticides on farmworkers, their families, and consumers. The documentary discussed the higher rates of cancer, birth defects, breathing disorders, and skin diseases in both consumers and farmworkers. For the next few years, Chávez went on speaking tours to talk about the dangers of pesticide use.

> *"If the union falls apart when I am gone, I will have been a miserable failure."*

Still Chávez felt that the speaking tours and education

Chávez launched another major boycott of grapes to call attention to the dangers of pesticides to both farmworkers and the public.

campaign were not enough. At midnight on the night of July 16, 1988, he began a fast to call attention to this issue. He called it the Fast for Life and refused to consume anything but water. He declined any contact with reporters. During the fast, Chávez attended a Catholic mass every day. He said that the fast "was for those who know they could or should do more. . . . The times we face truly call for all of us to do more to stop this evil in our midst."[4]

Actor Martin Sheen met Chávez during the fast and felt a great sense of calm and tears of joy spring to his eyes. The actor had just celebrated his forty-eighth birthday. Chávez, despite his weakened state, signed a black-and-red UFW flag and presented it to Sheen as a birthday gift.[5]

Although Chávez had fasted before, his friends and family were concerned for the sixty-one-year-old man. At the urging of his physicians, Chávez decided to stop. By the time he ended his thirty-six-day fast on August 21, he had lost thirty-three pounds. Toward the end of the fast, he became so physically weak that he had to whisper into people's ears to be heard. Doctors said that fasting had damaged Chávez's kidneys.[6]

Chávez broke his fast at a mass attended by thousands of supporters. He had to be carried in by two of his sons. Flanked by his wife and his ninety-six-year-old mother, Chávez looked frail. In attendance were Robert F. Kennedy's widow, Ethel, and the Kennedy children, as well as the Reverend Jesse Jackson.

A new fast was announced that day as well. Union supporters wanted to keep the fast going by taking turns for three days each. They would pass the small wooden cross that had become Chávez's symbol of the fast. The first person to take the cross and continue the fast was Jesse Jackson. Others who participated included entertainers Edward James Olmos, Martin Sheen, Emilio Estevez, Carly Simon, Danny Glover, and Whoopi Goldberg.

After he recuperated from the fast, Chávez traveled to New York City as part of his campaign against chemical use in the fields. While there, the unveiling of a computer-animated billboard in Times Square called *Pesticides* heartened him. Created by Barbara Carrasco, it dramatized the issue by showing a worker being sprayed by a crop duster while picking grapes. In the next scene, the grapes are bought by a woman in a supermarket. The grapes are taken home and eaten by children who then become ill. The animation ends with a *calavera*, a skull that traditionally represents death in Mexican culture. The billboard ran for a month to educate the public about pesticide use. Carrasco, the designer, had been nineteen when she first heard Chávez speak at the University of California at Los Angeles. After the speech, she volunteered her services

Through strikes, boycotts, rallies, and fasts, Chávez's commitment to *La Causa* never flagged.

to the union. Chávez accepted her offer, and Carrasco began painting banners for the union. As Chávez held a press conference at the unveiling of the billboard, Mayor David Dinkins raised the UFW flag over City Hall.

Chávez's fasting and the union's hard work were not in vain. By 1991, it was clear that consumers in major cities such as Los Angeles, New York, and San Francisco were buying significantly fewer grapes than before.[7]

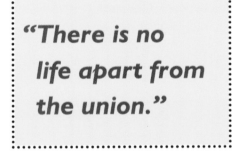

"There is no life apart from the union."

It was also in 1991 that Juana Chávez died at the age of ninety-nine. Her son César delivered a moving tribute to her life at Our Lady of Guadalupe Church in San Jose, California. Chávez was greatly saddened by his mother's death, and it took several months before he could summon up enough spirit to go back to work.

In the summer of 1992, Chávez led a march of ten thousand Salinas Valley farmworkers. They were protesting the poor conditions under which they worked.

On another front, Chávez was also disheartened by a court ruling. A company had sued the UFW for property damage sustained during one of the boycotts. The company won, and the UFW was ordered to pay $5.4 million. Disappointed by the judgment, the UFW filed an appeal.

Chávez traveled to San Luis, Arizona, in April 1993 to give testimony in the appeal. He chose to stay at the home of a farmworker and union supporter to bring attention to the situation, and he embarked on a fast. But Chávez did not look well, and friends convinced him on April 22 to end the fast. He agreed and went to bed in good spirits but exhausted.

On the morning of Thursday, April 23, 1993, sixty-six-year-old César Chávez was found dead. Medical examiners concluded that he had died peacefully in his sleep. Some people believe that too many fasts over the course of his lifetime had damaged Chávez's body.[8]

Chávez had once asked his brother Richard, who had worked as a carpenter, to build his coffin. Richard honored his brother's request of constructing a plain pine casket. It took two days to build.

Chávez had wanted his funeral to be held in Delano because of its importance for the union. On Sunday, April 26, family and close friends attended a private mass and viewing of the body. The California governor, Pete Wilson, ordered that all state flags be lowered to half-staff. Messages from heads of churches and states from around the world poured in. President Bill Clinton asked citizens to "reflect on and honor the life of this distinguished leader, veteran, and American."[9] Hillary Clinton, the first lady, sent a letter to Chávez's widow. Pope John Paul II sent his sympathies, which were later read at the funeral mass.

On the morning of the funeral, thirty-five thousand

This altar was set up to honor the farmworkers' leader.

to forty thousand people marched in ninety-degree heat in a three-mile funeral procession through Delano. The march ended at Forty Acres, where a mass was held. The body lay in state in the union hall, as mourners walked by to pay their respects. They had traveled from as far away as Toronto, Canada, and Miami, Florida. People missed work, and parents allowed children to skip school to attend the funeral. One grandfather lifted his grandson up to the coffin so that he could see Chávez's face, saying "See this man, I am going to tell you about him someday."[10]

Two of the marchers were Claudia and Robert Rosa. The brother and sister grew up going to picket lines with their parents, who were lawyers and activists in the farmworker movement. They had gotten to know Chávez personally, calling him Uncle César. "At the time, I didn't appreciate any of it," Claudia said. "I was a kid and I wanted to go to swim parties and do things with my friends, and some of them were children of big growers. Today, seeing all these people here, it is sinking in that my brother and I were part of something historic, something wonderful."[11]

The coffin was carried by Reverend Jesse Jackson, former California governor Jerry Brown, and some of Robert Kennedy's children. There were so many people who wanted to pay their respects by serving as pallbearers that the people carrying it changed every three minutes. Coretta Scott King, the widow of Martin Luther King, Jr., called Chávez "a rare and special kind of leader, completely devoid of ego, uninterested in the limelight and devoted to the cause of oppressed farmworkers."[12]

Wearing a *serape* (a woven shawl traditionally worn by Mexican men), Cardinal Roger M. Mahony led an outdoor mass in Spanish and English for the mourners in attendance. Chávez's twenty-seven grandchildren also took part in the ceremony. They placed a wooden carving of the UFW eagle and a *cortito* (short-handled hoe) on the altar, next to their grandfather's coffin. The eulogy was given by Dolores Huerta.

Luis Valdez and El Teatro Campesino gave a performance. Barbara Carrasco painted the banners for Chávez's funeral.

Celebrities including Edward James Olmos and Paul Rodriguez attended, as did Ethel Kennedy. One reporter asked Mrs. Kennedy, "César has been compared to your late husband Robert Kennedy and to Martin Luther King, Jr. What do you think of that?" Mrs. Kennedy replied, "Oh no, you can't do that, for you see, César was a saint."[13]

Chávez was buried in the rose garden in La Paz in a simple, private ceremony, as he had requested. Only his family and closest friends were present.

A journalist had once asked Chávez what motivated him to do his work as champion for the rights of farmworkers. Chávez told the reporter about how he had to quit school in the eighth grade to help his family by working full-time. He added, "I don't ever want to have another parent have to make the decisions that my parents made. That's why I'm doing this, and why I'm going to keep on doing this."[14]

To all those mourning César Chávez's death, it was evident that he had lived his life selflessly, always trying to improve the lives of others. He left huge shoes to fill, but he also left a legacy and a model for others to follow.

Chávez's Legacy

Juana Chávez, who had always loved *dichos*, or proverbs, would have been proud to hear a prominent California attorney compare her son to the pine tree in a famous *dicho*: "When a pine tree falls, it falls distributing millions of seeds that will one day create a stronger forest. César was our pine tree, we are his forest."[1]

It was César Chávez's fervent hope that subsequent generations would continue the work he had started. He felt confident that the movement would not lose momentum. In a speech, Chávez had said: "Once social change begins, it cannot be reversed. You cannot uneducate the person who has learned to read. You cannot humiliate the person who feels pride. You cannot oppress the people who are not afraid anymore."[2]

In April 1994, for the first anniversary of Chávez's death, more than eight hundred people completed a three-hundred-mile march across California. It was the

Family members, celebrities, and dignitaries marched to honor Chávez in 2003, the tenth anniversary of his death.

same route Chávez had taken in his 1966 pilgrimage from Delano to Sacramento. When they arrived in Sacramento, seventeen thousand farmworkers, union members, and supporters gathered with them at the state capitol. The president of the UFW, longtime UFW organizer Arturo Rodriguez, said, "César is not dead. Wherever farmworkers organize, stand up for their rights and fight for justice, César Chávez is with them. He is alive among us."[3]

Arturo S. Rodriguez

Arturo Rodriguez was a college student in 1969 when he became involved in the UFW's grape boycott. By 1971, he was organizing for the UFW. During a boycott in Michigan, Rodriguez met Linda Chávez, César's daughter. The two were married at La Paz in March 1974 and eventually had three children.

Rodriguez continued to organize boycotts and union elections and to teach others how to be union organizers. In 1981, he was elected to the UFW National Executive Board, and in 1993 he became the union's president. Rodriguez has worked hard to renew the union and increase its membership.

Linda Chávez died in October 2000 after a long illness.

In four states—Arizona, California, Colorado, and New Mexico—Chávez's birthday, March 31, has been designated as a state holiday. In California, it is a paid holiday for state employees.

On August 8, 1994, President Bill Clinton awarded Chávez the Presidential Medal of Freedom, the United States' highest civilian honor. Helen Chávez traveled to Washington, D.C., to receive the medal during a White House ceremony. Arturo Rodriguez, also in attendance, said, "Every day in California and in other states where farmworkers are organizing, César Chávez lives in their hearts. César lives wherever Americans he inspired work nonviolently for social change."[4]

Throughout his work, César Chávez held fast to his belief that the union must remain nonviolent. He said, "We are concerned with peace, because violence (and war is the worst type of violence) has no place in our society or in our world, and it must be eradicated."[5] Many credit Chávez with preventing injuries and even deaths. Lucío González, a California small businessman, said, "Others would have done things violently. The growers are lucky it was César who led the movement."[6]

Chávez tirelessly traveled the country, making speeches, influencing legislation, and educating the public. He often stayed in the homes of union supporters. A reporter once asked Chávez to speculate as to why so many farmworkers showed him so much affection and respect. Chávez smiled and simply replied, "The feeling is mutual."[7]

Chávez had a special relationship with children, too. One of his grandsons said that while Chávez was always involved in union activities, he still spent time with his grandchildren by including them: "When our friends would go with their grandfathers to a ball game, we would go with our grandfather to a demonstration. . . . When they would go to the store to buy food, we'd go there to picket and protest."[8]

On April 30, 1997, César Chávez was the first Latino to receive a plaque on the Latino Walk of Fame on Whittier Boulevard in Los Angeles. That same year, at the Sundance Film Festival, the documentary *The Fight in the Fields* premiered. The two filmmakers had personal and family ties to the UFW. Their two-hour film chronicled Chávez's life, the farmworkers' struggle, and also the Latino civil rights movement.

Fresno boasts the nation's first life-size statue of Chávez. Designed by sculptor Paul Suárez, the statue was installed at Fresno State University's Peace Garden on March 31, 1996, which would have been Chávez's sixty-ninth birthday. In 2003, on the tenth anniversary of Chávez's death, the United States Postal Service issued a postage stamp honoring the labor leader.

The César Chávez stamp was unveiled in Boston on April II, 2003.

Still, not everyone has been pleased with the commemorative events honoring Chávez's name. Some of California's growers continue to argue against naming streets and buildings after Chávez. When one grower heard that a local college was planning to name a new library after Chávez, he said, "We're not appreciative of naming anything after him."[9]

Debates have raged about having a national holiday for him, the state holiday in California, and several streets named after him. In San Francisco, there was a two-year debate about changing the Mission District's ARMY STREET to CÉSAR E. CHÁVEZ BOULEVARD. Although the name was officially changed, some protesters have put stickers proclaiming ARMY STREET over the street signs.

Thousands of farmworkers continue to remember Chávez's efforts through the services provided by the National Farmworkers Service Center (NFWSC). Soon after creating the farmworkers' labor union, Chávez founded the NFWSC to address farmworkers' health and housing needs. The NFWSC helps members with legal advice, immigration assistance, and medical needs. To date, it has built nearly one thousand homes and developed almost three thousand apartments for needy families. It also provides vocational training to farmworkers so they will have other employment options.

The NFWSC also manages a radio network for farmworkers across three states (California, Arizona, and Washington). Radio Campesino was another Chávez project, fulfilling his dream of reaching farmworkers in remote areas. President Carter's administration had made federal funds available to farmworker organizations. The UFW was granted modest start-up funds, and Radio Campesino was born.

When the radio station first went on the air in 1983, it had an all-talk format—serious discussions of worker abuses, legislation, and union activities. Listener surveys about the programming surprised its directors. Station director Anthony Chávez said, "People told us we were making their workday longer. They told us, 'Play some music.'"[10] In Phoenix, Arizona, it became the city's highest-rated Spanish-language radio station. Chávez's words could still be heard on the station each day at daybreak. The prayer, said in Spanish, had been written by Chávez in the early days of the UFW: "Lord, give me honesty and patience . . . so that we will never tire of the struggle."[11]

"If you want to remember me, organize!" César Chávez knew there would still be plenty of work to be done.

Soon after Chávez's death, his family and friends established the César E. Chávez Foundation to provide information about Chávez's life and work. In 2004, the foundation unveiled the César E. Chávez Education and Retreat

Center (CECERC) on 180 acres at La Paz. Built on a beautiful and serene setting, CECERC features three memorial and educational buildings. The memorial garden and visitor center graces Chávez's gravesite, which is marked by a simple wooden cross. The complex also features a museum, the home Chávez lived in for twenty years, his office, and many personal papers and possessions. Official union files and documents are archived at Wayne State University. A future building will be the focal point of summer youth camps designed to teach young people organizational and leadership skills.

The struggles continue. Sadly, even in the twenty-first century, the conditions under which migrant farmworkers toil and live continue to be appalling. Workers often do not have legal residency status—so they have no political clout—and eke out a bare existence. Many migrant farmworkers still live in cramped, inadequate housing with no running water or electricity. One investigation showed that workers in Florida were being paid only 40 cents for filling a thirty-two-pound bucket of tomatoes.[12] At a 1988 protest rally, Dolores Huerta was beaten badly enough by a police officer that she lost her spleen and had several ribs broken.

Despite these continuing challenges, Chávez's work and the UFW's influence have resulted in improvements such as medical services, retirement funds, and legal assistance for farmworkers.

Even today, migrant workers struggle to earn enough money to live on. The combined wages for this little boy and his mother came to about $30 for a whole day of picking green chilies.

One of the legacies of Chávez's work is Agbayani Village, a retirement home for elderly Filipino workers. Many of them had had no families. And because farm laborers were not eligible for Social Security benefits until the early 1970s, they were often destitute when they retired. Chávez had asked the UFW's executive board to approve the construction of a retirement home. The home was named after Paulo Agbayani, the Filipino worker who had died while on the picket line. It was constructed by volunteers on the original Forty

"All my life, I have been driven by one dream, one goal, one vision."

Acres site, and the first retirees moved into Agbayani Village in 1972.

In November 1984, Chávez gave a speech at the famous Commonwealth Club in San Francisco. The Commonwealth Club is the nation's oldest public affairs organization, dedicated to informing and debating about issues of public concern. Many famous people have spoken there, including Theodore Roosevelt, Martin Luther King, Jr., and Bill Clinton. In his speech, Chávez said: "All my life, I have been driven by one dream, one goal, one vision: To overthrow a farm labor system in this nation which treats farmworkers as if they were not important human beings. Farmworkers are not agricultural implements. They are not beasts of burden— to be used and discarded."[13]

César Chávez's life illustrates his motto, *Sí, se puede*. Through dedication and hard work, "Yes, it *can* be done." He has been credited with founding the most successful agricultural workers' union in U.S. history, and he served as UFW's president for three decades. Chávez's son Paul once said, "My father was a regular man, but he had a vision and he fought hard for it."[14] César Chávez's vision continues to inspire and provide a voice for farmworkers.

Artist Paul Suarez created this statue in Fresno, California.

Chronology

1927—César Estrada Chávez is born on March 31 near Yuma, Arizona.

1937—Chávez family moves to California.

1942—César quits school at the end of the eighth grade and becomes a full-time farmworker.

1944—Joins the U.S. Navy; is arrested in Delano, California, for sitting in the whites-only section of a segregated movie theater.

1948—Marries Helen Fabela on October 22.

1952—Meets community organizer Fred Ross in San Jose, California, and begins working for the Community Service Organization (CSO).

1962—Resigns from the CSO; moves to Delano, California, and with his associates creates the National Farmworkers Association (NFWA).

1965—The NFWA joins thousands of Filipino farmworkers in the Delano Grape Strike; the strike will last five years.

1966—Chávez leads a group of strikers on a 340-mile pilgrimage from Delano to the state capitol in Sacramento to draw national attention to the suffering of farmworkers; the first union contract between a grower and farmworkers' union in U.S. history is made; NFWA changes its name to the United Farmworkers (UFW).

1968—UFW calls for a national boycott of California table grapes; Chávez fasts for twenty-five days.

1974—Receives the Martin Luther King, Jr., Nonviolent Peace Prize.

1975—The Agricultural Labor Relations Act is enacted in California; *el cortito*, the short-handled hoe, is abolished.

1983—Radio Campesino begins broadcasting.

1986—*Wrath of Grapes* tour.

1988—Chávez's thirty-six-day Fast for Life draws attention to the table grape boycott; protests use of pesticides on grapes.

1993—César Chávez dies in his sleep on April 23.

1994—Awarded Presidential Medal of Freedom.

Chapter Notes

CHAPTER 1. "A LIVING SAINT"

1. David Gates, "A Secular Saint of the '60s," *Newsweek*, May 3, 1993, p. 68.
2. Stephanie Blondis Bower, in *Remembering Cesar*, compiled by Ann McGregor (Clovis, Calif.: Quill Driver Books, 2000), p. 28.
3. Harry Bernstein, "La Causa Lives," *Christianity and Crisis*, February 15, 1988, p. 35.
4. Jacques E. Levy, *Cesar Chavez: Autobiography of La Causa* (New York: Norton, 1975), p. 286.

CHAPTER 2. GROWING UP

1. Jacques E. Levy, *Cesar Chavez: Autobiography of La Causa* (New York: Norton, 1975), p. 18.
2. Ibid., p. 10.
3. Susan Ferriss and Ricardo Sandoval, *The Fight in the Fields* (New York: Harcourt Brace, 1997), p. 17.

CHAPTER 3. MIGRANT LIFE

1. Ronald Taylor, *Chavez and the Farmworkers* (Boston: Beacon Press, 1975), p. 61.
2. Peter Matthiessen, "Cesar Chavez," *The New Yorker*, May 17, 1993, p. 82.
3. Jacques E. Levy, *Cesar Chavez: Autobiography of La Causa* (New York: Norton, 1975), p. 65.

4. Taylor, p. 64.
5. Levy, p. 29.
6. Susan Ferriss and Ricardo Sandoval, *The Fight in the Fields* (New York: Harcourt Brace, 1997), p. 21.
7. Mark Arax and Jenifer Warren, "Chavez's Season of Gain for Farmworkers Slips Away," *Los Angeles Times*, April 29, 1993, p. 1.
8. Patt Morrison and Mark Arax, "For the Final Time, They March for Chavez Memorial," *Los Angeles Times*, April 30, 1993, p. 1.
9. Ferriss and Sandoval, p. 19.
10. Levy, p. 56.
11. Ibid., p. 48.
12. Dick Meister and Anne Loftis, *A Long Time Coming* (New York: Macmillan, 1977), p. 112.
13. Levy, p. 78.

CHAPTER 4. FINDING HIS WAY

1. Rodolfo Acuña, *Occupied America* (New York: Longman, 2000), p. 272.
2. Jacques E. Levy, *Cesar Chavez: Autobiography of La Causa* (New York: Norton, 1975), p. 84.

CHAPTER 5. ORGANIZING TO FIGHT INJUSTICE

1. Jacques E. Levy, *Cesar Chavez: Autobiography of La Causa* (New York: Norton, 1975), p. 99.
2. Dolores Huerta, "Reflection on the UFW Experience," *Center Magazine*, 1985, p. 2.

3. César Chávez, "The Organizer's Tale," in Renato Rosaldo et al., eds., *Chicano: The Evolution of a People* (Minneapolis: Winston Press, 1973), p. 298.
4. Huerta, p. 3.
5. Susan Ferriss and Ricardo Sandoval, *The Fight in the Fields* (New York: Harcourt Brace, 1997), p. 1.
6. Levy, p.5.
7. Bob and Liz Maxwell, in *Remembering Cesar*, compiled by Ann McGregor (Clovis, Calif.: Quill Driver Books, 2000), p. 24.
8. Michael Harrington, *The Other America* (New York: Simon & Schuster, 1962), p. 2.

CHAPTER 6. LA CAUSA IS BORN

1. Jacques E. Levy, *Cesar Chavez: Autobiography of La Causa* (New York: Norton, 1975), p. 197.
2. Mark Day, *Forty Acres* (New York: Praeger Publishers, 1971), p. 114.
3. César Chávez in Day, p. 9.
4. Dolores Huerta, "Reflection on the UFW Experience," *Center Magazine*, 1985, p. 8.
5. Rosa Maria Rodriguez and Arturo Villareal, "The UFW Strategies," *San Jose Studies*, Spring 1994, p. 66.
6. Huerta, p. 2.
7. Ibid., p. 3.
8. Andrés G. Guerrero, *A Chicano Theology* (Maryknoll, N.Y.: Orbis Books, 1987), p. 5.

9. Jessie De La Cruz, in *Remembering Cesar*, compiled by Ann McGregor (Clovis, Calif.: Quill Driver Books, 2000), p. 15.

10. Rosalyn Baxandall, Linda Gordon, and Susan Reverby, *America's Working Women* (New York: Random House, 1976), pp. 366–367.

11. Margaret Rose, "Traditional and Nontraditional Patterns of Female Activism in the United Farmworkers of America," *Frontiers*, 1990, p. 28.

12. Ibid., p. 29.

13. Ibid., p. 27.

14. Jerry Brown, in *Remembering Cesar*, p. 48.

15. Jose Angel Gutierrez, "César Chávez Estrada: The First and Last of the Chicano Leaders," *San Jose Studies 20(2)*, 1994, p. 34.

16. Rodriguez and Villareal, p. 65.

17. Susan Drake, "The El Andar Interview: Dolores Huerta," *El Andar*, December 2001, p. 20.

18. Colman McCarthy, "He Stood with the Field Hands," *The Washington Post*, May 1, 1993, p. A23.

19. Day, p. 156.

20. Levy, pp. 195–196.

21. David Gates, "A Secular Saint of the '60s," *Newsweek*, May 3, 1993, p. 68.

22. Samuel B. Trickey, in *Remembering Cesar*, p. 17.

23. Nicolaus Mills, "Remembering Cesar Chavez," *Dissent*, Fall 1993, p. 553.

24. Levy, p. 27.

25. Richard W. Etulain, ed., *César Chávez* (Boston: Bedford/ St. Martins, 2002), p. 70.
26. Larry Ruiz, "Chavez Stamp Unveiled," *La Prensa de San Antonio*, April 27, 2003, p. 1A.

CHAPTER 7. ¡HUELGA!

1. Susan Ferriss and Ricardo Sandoval, *The Fight in the Fields* (New York: Harcourt Brace, 1997), p. 98.
2. Dolores Huerta, "Reflection on the UFW Experience," *Center Magazine*, 1985, p. 4.
3. Bob and Liz Maxwell, in *Remembering Cesar*, compiled by Ann McGregor (Clovis, Calif.: Quill Driver Books, 2000), p. 24.
4. Jacques E. Levy, *Cesar Chavez: Autobiography of La Causa* (New York: Norton, 1975), p. 189.
5. Rosa Maria Rodriguez and Arturo Villareal, "The UFW Strategies," *San Jose Studies*, Spring 1994, p. 67.
6. Richard Steven Street, "The FBI's Secret File on César Chávez," *Southern California Quarterly*, 1998, p. 349.
7. Margaret Rose, "Traditional and Nontraditional Patterns of Female Activism in the United Farmworkers of America," *Frontiers*, 1990, p. 28.
8. Max Benavidez, "Cesar Chavez Nurtured Seeds of Art," *Los Angeles Times*, April 28, 1993, p. 1.
9. Angie Hernandez Herrera as quoted in Ferriss and Sandoval, p. 119.
10. Levy, p. 246.
11. Huerta, p. 4.

12. Mark Day, *Forty Acres* (New York: Praeger Publishers, 1971), p. 77.

CHAPTER 8. OPPOSITION

1. Jacques E. Levy, *Cesar Chavez: Autobiography of La Causa* (New York: Norton, 1975), pp. 292–293.
2. Richard Griswold del Castillo and Richard Garcia, "César Chávez: A Life of Courage, Struggle, and Commitment," *San Jose Studies 20(2)*, 1994, p. 25.
3. Colman McCarthy, "He Stood with the Field Hands," *The Washington Post*, May 1, 1993, p. A23.
4. Susan Ferriss and Ricardo Sandoval, *The Fight in the Fields* (New York: Harcourt Brace, 1997), p. 167.
5. Arturo S. Rodriguez, "Farmworkers Still Face Challenges 30 Years Later," *Mundo Hispanico*, September 2000, p. 44.
6. Levy, pp. 429, 432.
7. David Gates, "A Secular Saint of the '60s," *Newsweek*, May 3, 1993, p. 68.
8. Wayne Hartmire, in *Remembering Cesar*, compiled by Ann McGregor (Clovis, Calif.: Quill Driver Books, 2000), p. 22.
9. Frank Bardacke, "Cesar's Ghost," *The Nation*, July 26/August 2, 1993, p. 133.
10. Dolores Huerta, "Reflection on the UFW Experience," *Center Magazine*, 1985, p. 8.
11. Bob and Liz Maxwell, in *Remembering Cesar*, p. 24.
12. Peter Gines Velasco, in *Remembering Cesar*, p. 40.

13. Michael Kearney as quoted in Mark Arax and Jenifer Warren, "Chavez's Season of Gain for Farmworkers Slips Away," *Los Angeles Times*, April 29, 1993, p. 1.

14. Richard Griswold del Castillo, "Chávez: The Final Struggle," *Southern California Quarterly*, 1996, p. 206.

15. Bernice Powell Jackson, "Remembering Cesar Chavez," *Oakland Post*, April 30, 2003, p. 4.

16. Terry Vasquez Scott, in *Remembering Cesar*, p. 29.

17. Ferriss and Sandoval, p. 188.

CHAPTER 9. LATER YEARS

1. David Gates, "A Secular Saint of the '60s," *Newsweek*, May 3, 1993, p. 68.

2. Susan Ferriss and Ricardo Sandoval, *The Fight in the Fields* (New York: Harcourt Brace, 1997), p. 234.

3. Mark Day, *Forty Acres* (New York: Praeger Publishers, 1971), p. 64.

4. Arturo S. Rodriguez, in *Remembering Cesar*, compiled by Ann McGregor (Clovis, Calif.: Quill Driver Books, 2000), p. 12.

5. Martin Sheen, in *Remembering Cesar*, p. 100.

6. "Private Mass for Cesar Chavez's Family, Staff," *Oakland Tribune*, April 26, 1993, p. 4A.

7. Richard Griswold del Castillo, "Chávez: The Final Struggle," *Southern California Quarterly*, 1996, p. 210.

8. Jose Angel Gutierrez, "César Chávez Estrada: The First and Last of the Chicano Leaders," *San Jose Studies 20(2)*, 1994, p. 36.

9. Executive Order 6552, <envirotext.eh.doe.gov/data/eos/ clinton/19930428b.html> (March 11, 2004).

10. Patt Morrison and Mark Arax, "For the Final Time, They March for Chavez Memorial," *Los Angeles Times*, April 30, 1993, p. 1.

11. Ibid.

12. Coretta Scott King, in *Remembering Cesar*, p. 85.

13. Edward James Olmos, in *Remembering Cesar*, p. 16.

14. Paul Chávez as quoted in Ferriss and Sandoval, p. 268.

CHAPTER 10. CHÁVEZ'S LEGACY

1. Jose Padilla as quoted in Susan Ferriss and Ricardo Sandoval, *The Fight in the Fields* (New York: Harcourt Brace, 1997), p. 269.

2. "PBS Airs Chávez Documentary," <http://www. migrationint.com.au/ruralnews/greenland/> (March 21, 2004).

3. "More than 800 Supporters Join United Farmworkers," *La Voz de Colorado*, April 20, 1994, p. 15.

4. "CEC Story," <http://www.ufw.org/cecstory.htm> (June 20, 2003).

5. César Chávez in Mark Day, *Forty Acres* (New York: Praeger Publishers, 1971), p. 12.

6. Ferriss and Sandoval, p. 261.

7. Marc Grossman, in *Remembering Cesar*, compiled by Ann McGregor (Clovis, Calif.: Quill Driver Books, 2000), p. 4.

8. Juan Espinosa, "Descendant of Farm Leader Visits Pueblo, Colorado," *The Pueblo Chieftain*, March 25, 2002, p. XX.

9. Wes Bisgaard as quoted in Ferriss and Sandoval, p. 3.

10. Ingrid Lobet, "Righteous Brothers," *Mother Jones*, November, 2000, p. 24.

11. Ibid.

12. Bernice Powell Jackson, "Remembering Cesar Chavez," *Oakland Post*, April 30, 2003, p. 4.

13. Larry Ruiz, "Chavez Stamp Unveiled," *La Prensa de San Antonio*, April 27, 2003, p. 1A.

14. Ibid.

Further Reading

Brown, Jonatha A. *Cesar Chavez*. Milwaukee, Wisc.:
World Almanac Library, 2004.

Marcovitz, Hal. *Cesar Chavez*. Philadelphia, Pa.:
Chelsea House, 2003.

Matthews, J. L. *Cesar Chavez: Fighter in the Fields*.
Mankato, Minn.: Capstone Curriculum Publishing, 2002.

Ferriss, Susan, and Ricardo Sandoval. *The Fight in the Fields*.
New York: Harcourt Brace, 1997.

Seidman, David. *Cesar Chavez: Labor Leader*.
New York: Franklin Watts, 2004.

Soto, Gary. *César Chávez: A Hero for Everyone*.
New York: Alladin, 2003.

Tracy, Kathleen. *Cesar Chavez*. Bear, Del.:
Mitchell Lane, 2003.

Internet Addresses

César E. Chávez Institute, San Francisco State University
Interviews, speeches, photo gallery, links
<http://www.sfsu.edu/~cecipp/cesar_chavez/chavezhome.htm>

César E. Chávez Foundation
<http://www.cesarechavezfoundation.org>

César E. Chávez, County of Los Angeles Public Library
Biography, chronology, bibliography, links to sites in English and Spanish
<http://www.colapublib.org/chavez>

Index

Page numbers for photographs are in **boldface** type.